THE KILTARTAN BOOKS

The Coole Edition

General Editors
T. R. Henn, C.B.E., Litt.D.
Colin Smythe M.A.

Bronze bust of Lady Gregory by Epstein. Courtesy of the Municipal Gallery of Modern Art, Dublin.

THE KILTARTAN BOOKS
COMPRISING
THE KILTARTAN POETRY
HISTORY AND WONDER BOOKS
BY LADY GREGORY

Illustrated by
Robert and Margaret Gregory

with a foreword by
Padraic Colum

COLIN SMYTHE
GERRARDS CROSS
1971

This volume is published by Colin Smythe Ltd.,
Gerrards Cross, Bucks as the ninth volume
of the Coole Edition of Lady Gregory's works

SBN 900675 330

This volume is not for sale in the United States of America
where it is published by the Oxford University Press,
New York

333488

Printed and bound in Great Britain by
Hazell Watson & Viney Ltd at their Aylesbury works

FOREWORD

The Kiltartan Poetry Book, *The Kiltartan History Book* and *The Kiltartan Wonder Book* are in the language of the small, isolated houses and the open air. The people for whom it is habitual are not bookless, but the books they have read or that have been read to them would fit in a satchel; they have time for reveries and memories. Lady Gregory had a predecessor in the use of this medium—Douglas Hyde used it in translation of the Connacht songs. Lady Gregory herself made larger use of it in her narratives *Cuchulain of Muirthemne* and *Gods and Fighting Men*, and J. M. Synge used it with magnificent effect in his plays.

By title *The Kiltartan Poetry Book* spares us from thinking of it as an anthology: it is Irish poetry from long past and near present in the language of a parish. There are hundreds of years between the utterances, but they are not divided into epochs; there are the laments by princesses for famous husbands and the lament by a peasant girl for a brother hanged according to country law, and the language of a locality is used to bring both over to us. If we have some access to scholarship we will know that the ancient poems are in strict bardic metres, whereas his sister's lament for the young man hanged is in a metre familiar to the maker through verse that was never written down. This ignoring of forms and epochs reveals an underlying unity, an emotional continuity. The bereaved have been brought together, and we know them as kindred: their losses are for lifetime; they are aware of an external world; they know that the one for whom they lament has a hero's fame; for the peasant girl the hero's celebration will be his wake—"tobacco and pipes and white candles, and it will not be begrudged to them that will use it".

The Kiltartan History Book is about Kiltartan, that is to say about people of a parish of Galway. They are old people. "I am old enough to hear many histories," one says. Theirs is history becoming folklore.

It needs institutions to keep history factual or near factual, and in a bookless society actual happenings are made fit into some racial pattern: the story of Romulus and Remus and the foundation of Rome is, perhaps, an instance of this. One of the interesting things that comes to us from *The Kiltartan History Book* is the bias that this fitting-in takes: it is towards domesticity and family affection, I should say.

The story of Usheen's return to Ireland is not history—it is accepted tradition. He, the youngest of the heroes of the Fianna, is brought to the Land of Youth by an immortal woman. Three hundred years pass in continuous joy for him. Then he remembers the heroic companionship, and, ignorant of the passage of time, resolves to return to Ireland. Given a steed that will carry him over the waves, he is warned that if he sets foot upon native ground he can never return to the Land of Youth. In the accepted legend he comes to an Ireland whose lack of manly prowess can be perceived from the saddle. Men are bringing a stone for the building of a church, but they are a puny lot, flagging before they get anywhere. Contemptuously Usheen leans from his saddle to aid them. He touches the ground and becomes an old and feeble man. In the story told by Lady Gregory the hero is presented as the man of the cottages. The stone that brings him to the ground is not being transported: it is the trough outside the house where he and his brothers used to dwell, in which they used to wash themselves before they went into the fields with their spades. Overcome with memories he dismounts. Arrogance has become affection in the minds of the people who use the Kiltartan idiom.

The stories in *The Kiltartan Wonder Book* have a different genesis from the stories in the recognized collections of West of Ireland folk tales. They are told her by men and women whom Lady Gregory meets on the roads, sits with in wards of old-time workhouses or visits in their smoky cottages. They remember old stories for they have little else outside their own affairs to remember.

The stories in the collections and the stories in *The Kiltartan Wonder Book* are not interchangeable. The first pre-supposes a setting and a congregation. They are recitals. The setting is in some state before the peat fire, the congregation is to be entertained by a professional story teller. There is nothing casual about them as there may be in any of the wonders told to Lady Gregory, "Working all my life I am," exclaims one who is preparing to tell a story, "working with the flail in the barn, working with a spade at the potato tilling and the potato digging, breaking stones on the road, and four years ago the wife died, and it's lonesome to be in the house keeping alone." Persons are Lady Gregory's chief interest. They are not professionals, but they bring the mood of the listener, and sometimes a movement of a phrase that adds to what is in the record.

One of the stories is outside the type of traditional fireside recital—the Story of the Man who got rid of the Shadow that was Misfortune. It belongs to the type of Morality that was probably introduced by Preachers, and the one who diffused it obviously recognised that the predominant sin of the countryside was envy of another's prosperity: it is medieval. The traditional fireside recitals about Giants and Kings' sons and bespelled Brides are immemorial: this, though coming to us in the idiom of unlettered people is morally sophisticated.

How often I have noted that evocation of the Never-never Land:—

> Where the wind never blew nor the cocks never crew.

But it is one of Lady Gregory's non-professionals who completes the evocation for me:—

> Where the winds never blew
> Nor the cocks never crew,
> And the old boy himself never blew his horn.

The "old boy" being the Devil. *The Kiltartan Wonder Book* has persons in its foreground, and the wonders they relate are from personal memories of long-ago recitals. A listener can comment:— "Is there any meaning in the name Beswarragal?"

"Not a meaning; it is all the name she ever had, and it will be her name for ever and always."

The old wife of the man of a hundred years, who had fallen asleep listening, says to the old woman who was sitting on the doorstep, "Would you say there was any meaning in the name?" and she says, "I suppose she was just an enchanted woman." "Ah," says the old man, "I'll give you three words that will bring you to Heaven as easy as walking out into that street. And I will tell you now about the Seven Fishers." Persons! And how well they are brought over to us in all their originality!

PADRAIC COLUM

CONTENTS

The Kiltartan History Book

Some Broadsheet Ballads of the Wars

THE KILTARTAN POETRY BOOK

INTRODUCTION

I

IF in my childhood I had been asked to give the name of an Irish poem, I should certainly have said "Let Erin remember the days of old," or "Rich and rare were the gems she wore"; for although among the ornamental books that lay on the round drawingroom table, the only one of Moore's was *Lalla Rookh*, some guest would now and then sing one of his melodies at the piano; and I can remember vexing or trying to vex my governess by triumphant mention of Malachi's collar of gold, she no doubt as well as I believing the "proud invader" it was torn from to have been, like herself, an English one. A little later I came to know other verses, ballads nearer to the tradition of the country than Moore's faint sentiment. For a romantic love of country had awakened in me, perhaps through the wide beauty of my home, from whose hillsides I could see the mountain of Burren and Iar Connacht, and at sunset the silver western sea; or it maybe through the half revealed sympathy of my old nurse for the rebels whose cheering she remembered when the French landed at Killala in '98; or perhaps but through the natural breaking of a younger child of the house from the conservatism of her elders. So when we were taken sometimes as a treat the five mile drive to our market town, Loughrea, I would, on tiptoe at the counter, hold up the six pence earned by saying without a mistake my Bible lesson on the Sunday, and the old stationer, looking down through his spectacles would give me what I wanted saying that I was his best customer for Fenian books; and one of my sisters, rather doubtfully consented to my choice of *The Spirit of the Nation* for a birthday present, qualified the gift by copying into it "Patriotism is the last refuge of a scoundrel." I have some of them by me yet, the little books in gay paper or in green cloth, and some verses in them seem to me no less moving than in those early days, such as Davis's lament:

We thought you would not die, we were sure you would not go
And leave us in our utmost need to Cromwell's cruel blow;
Sheep without a shepherd when the snow shuts out the sky,
O why did you leave us Owen? Why did you die?

K.B.—2

And if some others are little more than a catalogue, unmusical, as:—

Now to begin to name them I'll continue in a direct line,
There's John Mitchell, Thomas Francis Meagher and also
  William Smith O'Brien;
John Martin and O'Donoghue, Erin sorely feels their loss,
And to complete their number I will include O'Donovan Ross—

yet there is in them a certain dignity, an intensity born of continuity of purpose; they are roughly hammered links in a chain of unequal workmanship, but stretching back through the centuries to the Munster poets of the days of Elizabeth, advised by Spenser to harry them out of Ireland. The names change from age to age, that is all. The verses of the seventeenth century hallow those of Mac Carthys and Fitzgeralds who fought for the Stuarts or "knocked obedience out of the Gall"; the eighteenth ended with the rebels of '98; the nineteenth had Emmet and Mitchell and its Manchester martyrs. Already in these early days of the twentieth the street singers cry out:

Mac Dermott, Mallin, Hanrahan, Daly, Colbert and Mac Bride
All men who for our country's cause have nobly bled and died.

Even Yeats, falling into the tradition, has put in a lyric the names of some of those who died in Easter week, and through whose death "a terribly beauty is born".

II

I am glad to remember that through the twelve years of our married life, 1880–92, my husband and his people were able to keep their liking and respect for each other. For those were the years of the land war, tenant struggling to gain a lasting possession for his children, landlord to keep that which had been given in trust to him for his; each ready in his anger to turn the heritage of the other to desolation; while the vision of some went yet farther, through breaking to the rebuilding of a nation. The passion, the imagination of Ireland were thrown into the fight. I often thought to find some poem putting such passion into fiery or memorable lines. But the first I thought worth the keeping—I have it yet—was Katherine Tynan's lament for Parnell, written two years after his death. In tearing it from the corner of some newspaper I had unwittingly taken note of almost the moment of a new impulse in literature, in poetry. For with that death, the loss of that dominant personality, and in the quarrel that followed, came the disbanding of an army, the unloosing of forces, the setting free of the imagination of Ireland.

III

Once in my childhood I had been eager to learn Irish; I thought to get leave to take lessons from an old Scripture-reader who spent a part of his time in the parish of Killinane, teaching such scholars as he could find to read their own language in the hope that they might turn to the only book then being printed in Irish, the Bible. But my asking, timid with the fear of mockery, was unheeded. Yet I missed but by a little an opportunity that might have made me a real Irish scholar, and not as I am imperfect, stumbling. For a kinsman learned in the language, the translator of the wonderful *Silva Gaedelica* had been sometimes a guest in the house, and would still have been welcomed there but that my mother, who had a great dislike to the marriage of cousins had fancied he was taking a liking to one of my elder sisters; and with that suspicion the "winged nymph, Opportunity" had passed from my reach. After my marriage I bought a grammar and worked at it for a while with the help of a gardener. But it was difficult and my teacher was languid, suspecting it may be some hidden mockery, for those were the days before Irish became the fashion. It was not till a dozen or more years later, and after my husband's death, that my son, having won the classical entrance scholarship at Harrow, took a fancy to learn a nearer language, and rode over to Tillyra before breakfast one morning to ask our neighbour Edward Martyn to help him to a teacher. He came back without what he had sought, but with the gift of a fine old Irish Bible, which became a help in our early lessons. For we set to work together, and I found the task a light one in comparison with those first attempts. For that young priest, Father Eugene O'Growney, sent from Ireland to look for health in California, had used the short space of life left to him in writing simple lessons in Irish grammar, that made at least the first steps easy. And another thing had happened. Dr. Douglas Hyde, *An Craoibhin*, had founded the Gaelic League, and through it country people were gathered together in the Irish speaking places to give the songs and poems, old and new, kept in their memory. This discovery, this disclosure of the folk learning, the folk poetry, the ancient tradition, was the small beginning of a weighty change. It was an upsetting of the table of values, an astonishing excitement. The imagination of Ireland had found a new homing place.

IV

My own imagination was aroused. I was becoming conscious of
a world close to me and that I had been ignorant of. It was not
now in the corners of newspapers I looked for poetic emotion,
nor even to the singers in the streets. It was among farmers and
potato diggers and old men in workhouses and beggars at my own
door that I found what was beyond these and yet farther beyond
that drawingroom poet of my childhood in the expression of love,
and grief, and the pain of parting, that are the disclosure of the
individual soul.

An Aran man, repeating to me *The Grief of a Girl's Heart* in
Irish told me it was with that song his mother had often sung him
to sleep as a child. It was from an old woman who had known Mary
Hynes and who said of her "The sun and the moon never shone
upon anything so handsome" that I first heard Raftery's song of
praise of her, "The pearl that was at Ballylee," a song "that has
gone around the world and as far as America." It was in a stone-
cutter's house where I went to have a headstone made for Raftery's
grave that I found a manuscript book of his poems, written out in
the clear beautiful Irish characters. It was to a working farmer's
house I walked on many a moonlit evening with the manuscript
that his greater knowledge helped me to understand and by his
hearth that I read for the first time the *Vision of Death* and the
Lament for O'Daly. After that I met with many old people who
had in the days before the Famine seen or talked with the wandering poet who was in the succession of those who had made and
recited their lyrics on the Irish roads before Chaucer wrote.

V

And so I came by the road nearest me to the old legends, the
old heroic poems. It was a man of a hundred years who told me
the story of Cuchulain's fight with his own son, the son of Aoife,
and how the young man as he lay dying had reproached him and
said "Did you not see how I threw every spear fair and easy at you,
and you threw your spear hard and wicked at me? And I did not
come out to tell my name to one or to two but if I had told it to
anyone in the whole world, I would soonest tell it to your pale
face." Deirdre's beauty "that brought the Sons of Usnach to their
death" comes into many of the country songs. Grania of the yet
earlier poems is not so well thought of. An old basket maker said
scornfully "Many would tell you she slept under the cromlechs
but I don't believe that, and she a king's daughter. And I don't
believe she was handsome, either. If she was, why would she have

run away?" And another said "Finn had more wisdom than all the men of the world, but he wasn't wise enough to put a bar on Grania." I was told in many places of Osgar's bravery and Goll's strength and Conan's bitter tongue, and the arguments of Oisin and Patrick. And I have often been given the story of Oisin's journey to Tir-nan-Og, the Country of the Young, that is, as I am told, "a fine place and everything that is good is in it. And if anyone is sent there for a minute he will want to stop in it, and twenty years will seem to him like one half hour"; and "they say Tir-nan-Og is there yet, and so it may be in any place."

VI

In the ancient times the poets told of this Country of the Young, with its trees bearing fruit and blossom at the one time; its golden apples that gave lasting life; its armies "that go out in good order, ahead of their beautiful king, marching among blue spears scattering their enemies, an army with high looks, rushing, avenging;" before news had come to Ireland, of the Evangelist's vision of the Tree of Life and of the "white horse, and he that sat on him had a bow, and a crown was given to him, and he went forth conquering and to conquer." They had told of the place "where delight is common, and music" before saintly Columcille on the night of the Sabbath of rest "reached to the troops of the archangels and the plain where music has not to be born." But in later days religion, while offering abundant pictures of an after world of punishment, "the flagstone of pain," "the cauldron that is boiling for ever," the fire the least flame of which is "bigger than fifteen hundred of turf," so that Oisin listening to St. Patrick demands a familiar weapon, an iron flail, to beat down such familiar terrors, has left Heaven itself far off, mysterious, intangible, without earthly similes or foreshadowings. I think it is perhaps because of this that the country poets of to-day and yesterday have put their dream, their vision of the Delectable Mountain, of the Land of Promise, into exaggerated praise of places dear to them. Raftery sees something beyond the barren Mayo bogs when he tells of that "fine place without fog falling, a blessed place that the sun shines on, and the wind does not rise there or anything of the sort," and where as he says in another poem "logwood and mahogany" grow in company with its wind twisted beech and storm bent sycamore. Even my own home "sweet Coole demesne" has been transfigured in songs of the neighbourhood; and a while ago an old woman asking alms at the door while speaking of a monastery near Athenry broke into a chant of praise that has in it perhaps some memory of the Well of Healing at the world's end that helped the gods to new strength in their great battle at Moytura. "Three barrels there are with water, and to see the first barrel boiling it is certain you will get a cure. Water there does be rushing down; you to stop you could hear it talking; to go there you would get cured of anything unless it might be the stroke of the Fool."

VII

In translating these poems I have chosen to do so in the speech of the thatched houses where I have heard and gathered them. *An Craoibhin* had already used this Gaelic construction, these Elizabethan phrases, in translating the *Love Songs of Connacht,* as I have used it even in my creative work. Synge had not yet used it when he found in my *Cuchulain of Muirthemne* "the dialect he had been trying to master," and of which he afterwards made such splendid use. Most of the translations in this book have already been printed in *Cuchulain of Muirthemne, Gods and Fighting Men, Saints and Wonders,* and *Poets and Dreamers.* When in the first month of the new year I began to choose from among them, it seemed strange to me that the laments so far outnumbered any songs of joy. But before that month was out news was brought to me that made the keening of women for the brave and of those who are left lonely after the young seem to be but the natural outcome and expression of human life.

AUGUSTA GREGORY

COOLE, May, 1918.

THE GRIEF OF A GIRL'S HEART

O DONALL og, if you go across the sea, bring myself with you and do not forget it; and you will have a sweetheart for fair days and market days, and the daughter of the King of Greece beside you at night. It is late last night the dog was speaking of you; the snipe was speaking of you in her deep marsh. It is you are the lonely bird through the woods; and that you may be without a mate until you find me.

You promised me, and you said a lie to me, that you would be before me where the sheep are flocked; I gave a whistle and three hundred cries to you, and I found nothing there but a bleating lamb.

You promised me a thing that was hard for you, a ship of gold under a silver mast; twelve towns with a market in all of them, and a fine white court by the side of the sea.

You promised me a thing that is not possible, that you would give me gloves of the skin of a fish; that you would give me shoes of the skin of a bird, and a suit of the dearest silk in Ireland.

O Donall og, it is I would be better to you than a high, proud, spendthrift lady: I would milk the cow; I would bring help to you; and if you were hard pressed, I would strike a blow for you.

O, ochone, and it's not with hunger or with wanting food, or drink, or sleep, that I am growing thin, and my life is shortened; but it is the love of a young man has withered me away.

It is early in the morning that I saw him coming, going along the road on the back of a horse; he did not come to me; he made nothing of me; and it is on my way home that I cried my fill.

When I go by myself to the Well of Loneliness, I sit down and I go through my trouble; when I see the world and do not see my boy, he that has an amber shade in his hair.

It was on that Sunday I gave my love to you; the Sunday that is last before Easter Sunday. And myself on my knees reading the Passion; and my two eyes giving love to you for ever.

O, aya! my mother, give myself to him; and give him all that you have in the world; get out yourself to ask for alms, and do not come back and forward looking for me.

My mother said to me not to be talking with you to-day, or to-morrow, or on the Sunday; it was a bad time she took for telling me that; it was shutting the door after the house was robbed.

My heart is as black as the blackness of the sloe, or as the black coal that is on the smith's forge; or as the sole of the shoe left in white halls; it was you put that darkness over my life.

You have taken the east from me; you have taken the west from me; you have taken what is before me and what is behind me; you have taken the moon, you have taken the sun from me; and my fear is great that you have taken God from me!

A LAMENT FOR FAIR-HAIRED DONOUGH
THAT WAS HANGED IN GALWAY

Iт was bound fast here you saw him, and wondered to see him,
Our fair-haired Donough, and he after being condemned;
There was a little white cap on him in place of a hat,
And a hempen rope in the place of a neck-cloth.

I am after walking here all through the night,
Like a young lamb in a great flock of sheep;
My breast open, my hair loosened out,
And how did I find my brother but stretched before me!

The first place I cried my fill was at the top of the lake;
The second place was at the foot of the gallows;
The third place was at the head of your dead body
Among the Gall, and my own head as if cut in two.

If you were with me in the place you had a right to be,
Down in Sligo or down in Ballinrobe,
It is the gallows would be broken, it is the rope would be cut
And fair-haired Donough going home by the path.

O fair-haired Donough, it is not the gallows was fit for you;
But to be going to the barn; to be threshing out the straw;
To be turning the plough to the right hand and to the left,
To be putting the red side of the soil uppermost.

O fair-haired Donough, O dear brother,
It is well I know who it was took you away from me;
Drinking from the cup, putting a light to the pipe,
And walking in the dew in the cover of the night.

O Michael Malley, O scourge of misfortune!
My brother was no calf of a vagabond cow;
But a well-shaped boy on a height or a hillside,
To knock a low pleasant sound out of a hurling-stick.

And fair-haired Donough, is not that the pity,
You that would carry well a spur or a boot;
I would put clothes in the fashion on you from cloth that
    would be lasting;
I would send you out like a gentleman's son.

O Michael Malley, may your sons never be in one another's
    company;
May your daughters never ask a marriage portion of you;
The two ends of the table are empty, the house is filled,
And fair-haired Donough, my brother, is stretched out.

There is a marriage portion coming home for Donough,
But it is not cattle or sheep or horses;
But tobacco and pipes and white candles,
And it will not be begrudged to them that will use it.

RAFTERY'S PRAISE OF MARY HYNES

GOING to Mass by the will of God, the day came wet and the wind rose; I met Mary Hynes at the cross of Kiltartan, and I fell in love with her there and then.

I spoke to her kind and mannerly, as by report was her own way; and she said "Raftery my mind is easy; you may come to-day to Ballylee."

When I heard her offer I did not linger; when her talk went to my heart my heart rose. We had only to go across the three fields; we had daylight with us to Ballylee.

The table was laid with glasses and a quart measure; she had fair hair and she sitting beside me; and she said, "Drink, Raftery, and a hundred welcomes; there is a strong cellar in Ballylee."

O star of light and O sun in harvest; O amber hair, O my share of the world! Will you come with me on the Sunday, till we agree together before all the people?

I would not begrudge you a song every Sunday evening; punch on the table or wine if you would drink it. But O King of Glory, dry the roads before me till I find the way to Ballylee.

There is sweet air on the side of the hill, when you are looking down upon Ballylee; when you are walking in the valley picking nuts and blackberries, there is music of the birds in it and music of the Sidhe.

What is the worth of greatness till you have the light of the flower of the branch that is by your side? There is no good to deny it or to try and hide it; she is the sun in the heavens who wounded my heart.

There was no part in Ireland I did not travel, from the rivers to the tops of the mountains; to the edge of Lough Greine whose mouth is hidden, and I saw no beauty but was behind hers.

Her hair was shining and her brows were shining too; her face was like herself, her mouth pleasant and sweet; She is the pride and I give her the branch; she is the shining flower of Ballylee.

It is Mary Hynes, the calm and easy woman, has beauty in her mind and in her face. If a hundred clerks were gathered together, they could not write down a half of her ways.

HIS LAMENT FOR O'DALY

IT was Thomas O'Daly that roused up young people and scattered them, and since death played on him, may God give him grace. The country is all sorrowful, always talking, since their man of sport died that would win the goal in all parts with his music. The swans on the water are nine times blacker than a blackberry since the man died from us that had pleasantness on the top of his fingers. His two grey eyes were like the dew of the morning that lies on the grass. And since he was laid in the grave, the cold is getting the upper hand.

If you travel the five provinces, you would not find his equal for countenance or behaviour, for his equal never walked on land or grass. High King of Nature, you who have all powers in yourself, he that wasn't narrow-hearted, give him shelter in heaven for it!

He was the beautiful branch. In every quarter that he ever knew he would scatter his fill and not gather. He would spend the estate of the Dalys, their beer and their wine. And that he may be sitting in the chair of grace, in the middle of Paradise!

A sorrowful story on death, it's he is the ugly chief that did treachery, that didn't give him credit, O strong God, for a little time.

There are young women, and not without reason, sorry and heart-broken and withered, since he was left at the church. Their hair thrown down and hanging, turned grey on their head.

No flower in any garden, and the leaves of the trees have leave to cry, and they falling on the ground. There is no green flower on the tops of the tufts, since there did a boarded coffin go on Daly.

There is sorrow on the men of mirth, a clouding over the day, and no trout swim in the river. Orpheus on the harp, he lifted up everyone out of their habits; and he that stole what Argus was watching the time he took away Io; Apollo, as we read, gave them teaching, and Daly was better than all these musicians.

A hundred wouldn't be able to put together his actions and his deeds and his many good works. And Raftery says this much for Daly, because he liked him.

HIS PRAISE OF THE LITTLE HILL AND
THE PLAINS OF MAYO

AFTER the Christmas, with the help of Christ, I will never stop
if I am alive; I will go to the sharp-edged little hill; for it is a
fine place without fog falling; a blessed place that the sun shines
on, and the wind doesn't rise there or anything of the sort.

And if you were a year there you would get no rest, only sitting
up at night and forever drinking.

The lamb and the sheep are there; the cow and the calf are
there, fine lands are there without heath and without bog. Ploughing and seeding in the right month, plough and harrow prepared
and ready; the rent that is called for there, they have means to
pay it. There is oats and flax and large eared barley. There are
beautiful valleys with good growth in them and hay. Rods grow
there, and bushes and tufts, white fields are there and respect for
trees; shade and shelter from wind and rain; priests and friars
reading their book; spending and getting is there, and nothing
scarce.

I leave it in my will that my heart rises as the wind rises, and
as the fog scatters, when I think upon Carra and the two towns
below it, on the two-mile bush and on the plains of Mayo. And
if I were standing in the middle of my people, age would go from
me and I would be young again.

HIS LAMENT FOR O'KELLY

THERE'S no dew or grass on Cluan Leathan. The cuckoo is not to be seen on the furze; the leaves are withering and the trees complaining of the cold. There is no sun or moon in the air or in the sky, or no light in the stars coming down, with the stretching of O'Kelly in the grave.

My grief to tell it! he to be laid low; the man that did not bring grief or trouble on any heart, that would give help to those that were down.

No light on the day like there was; the fruits not growing; no children on the breast; there's no return in the grain; the plants don't blossom as they used since O'Kelly with the fair hair went away; he that used to forgive us a great share of the rent. Since the children of Usnach and Deirdre went to the grave, and Cuchulain, who as the stories tell us, would gain victory in every step he would take; since he died such a story never came of sorrow or defeat; since the Gael were sold at Aughrim, and since Owen Roe died, the Branch.

HIS VISION OF DEATH

I HAD a vision in my sleep last night between sleeping and waking. A figure standing beside me, thin, miserable, sad and sorrowful; the shadow of night upon his face, the tracks of the tears down his cheeks. His ribs were bending like the bottom of a riddle; his nose thin that it would go through a cambric needle; his shoulders hard and sharp that they would cut tobacco; his head dark and bushy like the top of a hill; and there is nothing I can liken his fingers to. His poor bones without any kind of covering; a withered rod in his hand, and he looking in my face. . . .

Death is a robber who heaps together kings, high princes and country lords; he brings with him the great, the young, and the wise, gripping them by the throat before all the people. Look at him who was yesterday swift and strong, who would leap stone wall, ditch and gap. Who was in the evening walking the street, and is going under the clay on the morrow.

It is a pity for him that is tempted with the temptations of the world; and the store that will go with him is so weak, and his lease of life no better if he were to live for a thousand years than just as if he had slipped over on a visit and back again.

When you are going to lie down don't be dumb. Bare your knee and bruise the ground. Think of all the deeds that you put by you, and that you are travelling towards the meadow of the dead.

HIS REPENTANCE

O KING who art in Heaven, I scream to Thee again and aloud, for it is Thy grace I am hoping for.

I am in age and my shape is withered; many a day I have been going astray. When I was young my deeds were evil; I delighted greatly in quarrels and rows. I liked much better to be playing or drinking on a Sunday morning than to be going to Mass. I was given to great oaths, and I did not let lust or drunkenness pass me by.

The day has stolen away and I have not raised the hedge, until the crop in which Thou didst take delight is destroyed. I am a worthless stake in the corner of a hedge, or I am like a boat that has lost its rudder, that would be broken against a rock in the sea, and that would be drowned in the cold waves.

HIS ANSWER WHEN SOME STRANGER
ASKED WHO HE WAS

I AM Raftery the poet, full of hope and love; my eyes without light, my gentleness without misery. Going west on my journey with the light of my heart; weak and tired to the end of my road.

I am now, and my back to a wall, playing music to empty pockets.

34

A BLESSING ON PATRICK SARSFIELD

O PATRICK SARSFIELD, health be to you, since you went to France and your camps were loosened; making your sighs along with the king, and you left poor Ireland and the Gael defeated—Och ochone! O Patrick Sarsfield, it is a man with God you are; and blessed is the earth you ever walked on. The blessing of the bright sun and the moon upon you, since you took the day from the hands of King William—Och ochone!

O Patrick Sarsfield, the prayer of every person with you; my own prayer and the prayer of the Son of Mary with you, since you took the narrow ford going through Biorra, and since at Cuilenn O'Cuanac you won Limerick—Och ochone!

I will go up on the mountain alone; and I will come hither from it again. It is there I saw the camp of the Gael, the poor troop thinned, not keeping with one another—Och ochone!

My five hundred healths to you, halls of Limerick, and to the beautiful troop was in our company; it is bonefires we used to have and playing-cards, and the word of God was often with us— Och ochone!

There were many soldiers glad and happy, that were going the way through seven weeks; but now they are stretched down in Aughrim—Och ochone!

They put the first breaking on us at the bridge of the Boyne; the second breaking on the bridge of Slaine; the third breaking in Aughrim of O'Kelly; and O sweet Ireland, my five hundred healths to you—Och ochone!

O'Kelly has manuring for his land, that is not sand or dung, but ready soldiers doing bravery with pikes, that were left in Aughrim stretched in ridges—Och ochone!

Who is that beyond on the hill, Ben Edair? I a poor soldier with King James. I was last year in arms and in dress, but this year I am asking alms—Och ochone!

AN ARAN MAID'S WEDDING

I AM widow and maid, and I very young; did you hear my great grief, that my treasure was drowned? If I had been in the boat that day, and my hand on the rope, my word to you, O'Reilly, it is I would have saved you sorrow.

Do you remember the day the street was full of riders, and of priests and brothers, and all talking of the wedding feast? The fiddle was there in the middle, and the harp answering to it; and twelve mannerly women to bring my love to his bed.

But you were of those three that went across to Kilcomin, ferrying Father Peter, who was three-and-eighty years old; if you came back within a month itself, I would be well content; but is it not a pity I to be lonely, and my first love in the waves?

I would not begrudge you, O'Reilly, to be kinsman to a king; white bright courts around you, and you lying at your ease; a quiet, well-learned lady to be settling out your pillow; but it is a great thing you to die from me when I had given you my love entirely.

It is no wonder a broken heart to be with your father and your mother; the white-breasted mother that crooned you, and you a baby; your wedded wife, O thousand treasures, that never set out your bed; and the day you went to Trabawn, how well it failed you to come home.

Your eyes are with the eels, and your lips with the crabs; and your two white hands under the sharp rule of the salmon. Five pounds I would give to him that would find my true love. Ochone! it is you are a sharp grief to young Mary ni-Curtain!

A POEM WRITTEN IN TIME OF TROUBLE BY AN IRISH PRIEST WHO HAD TAKEN ORDERS IN FRANCE

My thoughts, my grief! are without strength
My spirit is journeying towards death
My eyes are as a frozen sea
My tears my daily food;
There is nothing in life but only misery.
My poor heart is torn
And my thoughts are sharp wounds within me,
Mourning the miserable state of Ireland.

Misfortune has come upon us all together
The poor, the rich, the weak and the strong
The great lord by whom hundreds were maintained
The powerful strong man, and the man that holds the plough;
And the cross laid on the bare shoulder of every man.

Our feasts are without any voice of priests
And none at them but women lamenting
Tearing their hair with troubled minds
Keening miserably after the Fenians.

The pipes of our organs are broken
Our harps have lost their strings that were tuned
That might have made the great lamentations of Ireland.
Until the strong men come back across the sea
There is no help for us but bitter crying,
Screams, and beating of hands, and calling out.

I do not know of anything under the sky
That is friendly or favourable to the Gael
But only the sea that our need brings us to,
Or the wind that blows to the harbour
The ship that is bearing us away from Ireland;
And there is reason that these are reconciled with us,
For we increase the sea with our tears
And the wandering wind with our sighs.

THE HEART OF THE WOOD

My hope and my love, we will go for a while into the wood, scattering the dew, where we will see the trout, we will see the blackbird on its nest; the deer and the buck calling, the little bird that is sweetest singing on the branches; the cuckoo on the top of the fresh green; and death will never come near us for ever in the sweet wood.

AN CRAOIBHIN COMPLAINS BECAUSE
HE IS A POET

IT's my grief that I am not a little white duck,
And I'd swim over the sea to France or to Spain;
I would not stay in Ireland for one week only,
To be without eating, without drinking, without a full jug.

Without a full jug, without eating, without drinking,
Without a feast to get, without wine, without meat,
Without high dances, without a big name, without music;
There is hunger on me, and I astray this long time.

It's my grief that I am not an old crow,
I would sit for awhile up on the old branch;
I could satisfy my hunger, and I not as I am
With a grain of oats or a white potato.

It's my grief that I am not a red fox,
Leaping strong and swift on the mountains,
Eating cocks and hens without pity,
Taking ducks and geese as a conquerer.

It's my grief that I am not a bright salmon,
Going through the strong full water,
Catching the mayflies by my craft,
Swimming at my choice and swimming with the stream.

It's my grief that I am of the race of the poets;
It would be better for me to be a high rock,
Or a stone or a tree or an herb or a flower
Or anything at all but the thing that I am!

HE CRIES OUT AGAINST LOVE

THERE are three fine devils eating my heart—
They left me, my grief! without a thing;
Sickness wrought, and Love wrought,
And an empty pocket, my ruin and my woe.
Poverty left me without a shirt,
Barefooted, barelegged, without any covering;
Sickness left me with my head weak
And my body miserable, an ugly thing.
Love left me like a coal upon the floor,
Like a half-burned sod that is never put out.
Worse than the cough, worse than the fever itself,
Worse than any curse at all under the sun,
Worse than the great poverty
Is the devil that is called "Love" by the people.
And if I were in my young youth again
I would not take, or give, or ask for a kiss!

HE MEDITATES ON THE LIFE OF A
RICH MAN

A GOLDEN cradle under you, and you young;
A right mother and a strong kiss.

A lively horse, and you a boy;
A school and learning and close companions.

A beautiful wife, and you a man;
A wide house and everything that is good.

A fine wife, children, substance;
Cattle, means, herds and flocks.

A place to sit, a place to lie down;
Plenty of food and plenty of drink.

After that, an old man among old men;
Respect on you and honour on you.

Head of the court, of the jury, of the meeting,
And the counsellors not the worse for having you.

At the end of your days death, and then
Hiding away; the boards and the church.

What are you better after to-night
Than Ned the beggar or Seaghan the fool?

FORGAILL'S PRAISE OF COLUMCILLE

THIS now is the poem of praise and of lamentation that was made for Columcille, Speckled Salmon of the Boyne, High Saint of the Gael, by Forgaill that was afterwards called Blind Forgaill, Chief Poet of Ireland:

It is not a little story this is; it is not a story about a fool it is; it is not one district that is keening but every district with a great sound that is not to be borne, hearing the story of Columcille, without life, without a church.

It is not the trouble of one house, or the grief of one harp-string; all the plains are heavy, hearing the word that is a wound.

What way will a simple man tell of him? Even Nera from the Sidhe could not do it; he is not made much of now; our learned one is not the light of our life, now he is hidden away from us.

He that used to keep us living is dead; he that was our rightful head has died from us; he has died from us that was God's messenger.

The knowledgeable man that used to put fear from us is not here; the teller of words does not return to us; the teacher is gone from us that taught silence to the people.

The whole world was his; it is a harp without its strings; it is a church without its abbot.

Colum rose very high the time God's companies rose to meet him; it is bright the angels were, attending on him.

It is short his life was, it is little used to satisfy him; when the wind blew the sheet against him on the sand, the shape of his ribs could be seen through it. He was the head of every gathering; he was a dun of the book of the law; he put a flame in the district of the north, he lightened the district of the west; the east was his along with it: he did not open his heart to every company. Good his death; he went with God's angels that came to meet him.

He has reached to Axal of his help and to the troops of the arch-angels; he has reached to a place where night is not seen; he has reached to a plain where music has not to be born; where no one listens to oppression. The King of priests has done away with his troubles.

He knew the way he was going; he gave kindness for hatred; he learned psalms; he broke the battle against hunger.

He knew seasons and storms; he read the secrets of the great wisdom; he knew the course of the moon; he took notice of its race with the branching sun. He was skilful in the course of the sea; to tell every high thing we have heard from Colum, would be to count the stars of heaven.

A healer of the heart of the wise; a full satisfier of guests; our crowned one who spoke with Axal; a shelter to the naked; a comforter to the poor; he was eager, he was noble, it is high his death was. We hope great honour will be given to him on the head of these deeds.

And when Forgaill had made that lament he said, "It is a great shaping and a great finish I have given to these words, and I cannot make a praise beyond this, for my eyes have been taken from me."

It was Aodh, King of Ireland gave seven cumhals for his name to be given in the praising of Columcille; and Aodh laid it down to Forgaill that this song should be above every other song.

But it was after death the reward and the praise were given to blind Forgaill for it was Heaven that was given to him as the price of the praising of the King.

THE DEER'S CRY

BLESSED Patrick made this hymn one time he was going to preach the Faith at Teamhuir, and his enemies lay in hiding to make an attack on him as he passed. But all they could see passing as he himself and Benen his servant went by, was a wild deer and a fawn. And the Deer's Cry is the name of the hymn to this day.

I bind myself to-day to a strong strength, to a calling on the Trinity. I believe in a Threeness with confession of a Oneness in the Creator of the World.

I bind myself to-day to the strength of Christ's birth and His baptism; to the strength of His crucifixion with His burial; to the strength of His resurrection with His ascension;

In stability of earth, in steadfastness of rock, I bind to myself to-day God's strength to pilot me;

God's power to uphold me; God's wisdom to guide me; God's eye to look before me; God's ear to hear me;

God's word to speak for me; God's hand to guard me; God's path to lie before me: God's shield to protect me; God's host to save me;

Against snares of demons; against the begging of sins; against the asking of nature; against all my ill-wishers near me and far from me; alone and in a crowd.

So I have called on all these strengths to come between me and every fierce and merciless strength that may come between my body and my soul;

Again incantations of false prophets; against black laws of heathens; against false laws of heretics; against craft of idolatry; against spells of women and smiths and druids; against every knowledge forbidden to the souls of men.

Christ for my protection to-day against poison, against burning, against drowning, against wounding; that a multitude of rewards may come to me. Christ with me, Christ before me; Christ behind me, Christ in me; Christ under me, Christ over me; Christ to the right of me, Christ to the left of me; Christ in lying down, Christ in sitting, Christ in rising up;

Christ in the heart of everyone that thinks of me; Christ in the mouth of everyone that speaks to me; Christ in every eye that sees me; Christ in every ear that hears me.

I bind to myself to-day a strong strength to a calling upon the Trinity; I believe in a Threeness with confession of a Oneness in the Creator of the World.

THE HYMN OF MOLLING'S GUEST,
THE MAN FULL OF TROUBLE

HE is clean gold, he is Heaven about the sun, he is a silver vessel having wine in it: he is an angel, he is the wisdom of saints; everyone that is doing the will of the King.

He is a bird with a trap closing about him; he is a broken ship in great danger; he is an empty vessel, he is a withered tree; he that is not doing the will of the King.

He is a sweet-smelling branch with its blossoms; he is a vessel that is full of honey; he is a shining stone of good luck; he who does the will of the Son of God of Heaven.

He is a blind nut without profit; he is ill-smelling rottenness, he is a withered tree; he is a wild apple branch without blossom; he that is not doing the will of the King.

If he does the will of the Son of God of Heaven, he is a bright sun with summer about it; he is the image of the God of Heaven; he is a vessel of clear glass.

He is a racehorse over a smooth plain, the man that is striving for the kingdom of the great God; he is a chariot that is seen under a king, that wins the victory with golden bridles.

He is a sun that warms high heaven; the king to whom the great King is thankful; he is a church, joyful, noble; he is a shrine having gold about it.

He is an altar having wine poured upon it; having many quires singing around; he is a clean chalice with ale in it; he is bronze, white, shining, he is gold.

THE HAG OF BEARE

IT is of Corca Dubhne she was, and she had her youth seven times over, and every man that had lived with her died of old age, and her grandsons and great-grandsons were tribes and races. And through a hundred years she wore upon her head the veil Cuimire had blessed. Then age and weakness came upon her and it is what she said:

Ebb-tide to me as to the sea; old age brings me reproach; I used to wear a shift that was always new; to-day, I have not even a cast one.

It is riches you are loving, it is not men; it was men we loved in the time we were living.

There were dear men on whose plains we used to be driving; it is good the time we passed with them; it is little we were broken afterwards.

When my arms are seen it is long and thin they are; once they used to be fondling, they used to be around great kings.

The young girls give a welcome to Beltaine when it comes to them; sorrow is more fitting for me; an old pitiful hag.

I have no pleasant talk; no sheep are killed for my wedding; it is little but my hair is grey; it is many colours I had over it when I used to be drinking good ale.

I have no envy against the old, but only against women; I myself am spent with old age, while women's heads are still yellow.

The stone of the kings on Feman; the chair of Ronan in Bregia; it is long since storms have wrecked them, they are old mouldering gravestones.

The wave of the great sea is speaking; the winter is striking us with it; I do not look to welcome to-day Fermuid son of Mugh.

I know what they are doing; they are rowing through the reeds of the ford of Alma; it is cold is the place where they sleep.

The summer of youth where we were has been spent along with its harvest; winter age that drowns everyone, its beginning has come upon me.

It is beautiful was my green cloak, my king liked to see it on me; it is noble was the man that stirred it, he put wool on it when it was bare.

Amen, great is the pity; every acorn has to drop. After feasting with shining candles, to be in the darkness of a prayer-house.

I was once living with kings, drinking mead and wine; to-day I am drinking whey-water among withered old women.

There are three floods that come up to the dun of Ard-Ruide: a flood of fighting-men, a flood of horses, a flood of the hounds of Lugaidh's son.

The flood-wave and the two swift ebb-tides; what the flood-wave brings you in, the ebb-wave sweeps out of your hand.

The flood-wave and the second ebb-tide; they have all come as far as me, the way that I know them well.

The flood-tide will not reach to the silence of my kitchen; though many are my company in the darkness, a hand has been laid upon them all.

My flood-tide! It is well I have kept my knowledge. It is Jesus Son of Mary keeps me happy at the ebb-tide.

It is far is the island of the great sea where the flood reaches after the ebb: I do not look for floods to reach to me after the ebb-tide.

There is hardly a little place I can know again when I see it; what used to be on the flood-tide is all on the ebb to-day!

Some of the Wonders told at the Great Gathering in the East of the World by the Voice of Philip the Apostle, that was like the Laughter of an Army, and with that no louder than the Talk of Friend in the Ear of Friend;

I. THE SEVEN HEAVENS

As to the Seven Heavens that are around the earth, the first of them is the bright cloudy heaven that is the nearest and that has shining out of it the moon and the scattering of stars. Beyond that are two flaming heavens, angels are in them and the breaking loose of winds. Beyond those an ice-cold heaven, bluer than any blue, seven times colder than any snow, and it is out of that comes the shining of the sun. Two heavens there are above that again, bright like flame, and it is out of them shine the fiery stars that put fruitfulness in the clouds and in the sea. A high heaven, high and fiery, there is above all the rest; highest of all it is, having within it the rolling of the skies, and the labour of music, and quires of angels. In the belts, now, of the seven heavens are hidden the twelve shaking beasts that have fiery heads upon their heavenly bodies and that are blowing twelve winds about the world.

In the same belts are sleeping the dragons with fiery breath, tower-headed, blemished, that give out the crash of the thunders and blow lightnings out of their eyes.

II. THE JOURNEY OF THE SUN

GOD made on the fourth day the two and seventy kinds of the wandering stars of heaven, and the fiery course of the sun that warms the world with the sense and the splendour of angels.

Twelve plains there are under the body of the earth he lightens every night; the fiery sea laughs against his journey; ranks of angels come together, welcoming his visit after the brightness of the night. The first place he brightens is the stream beyond the seas, with news of the eastern waters. Then he lightens the ocean of fire and the seas of sulphur-fire that are round about the red countries.

Then he shines upon the troops of boys in the pleasant fields, who send out their cry to heaven through dread of the beast that kills thousands of armies under the waves of the south. Then he shines upon the mountains that have streams of fire, on the hosts that protect them in the plains. Then the ribs of the great beast shine, and the four and twenty champions rise up in the valley of pain. He shines over against the terrible many-thronged fence in the north that has closed around the people of hell. He shines on the dark valleys having sorrowful streams over their faces. He brightens the ribs of the beast that sends out the many seas around the earth; that sucks in again the many seas till the sands on every side are dry. He shines upon the many beasts that sleep their sleep of tears in the valley of flowers from the first beginning of the world; and on the sorrowful tearful plain, with the dragons that were set under the mist. He shines then upon the bird-flocks singing their many tunes in the flower-valleys; upon the shining plains with the wine-flowers that lighten the valley; he shines at the last against Adam's Paradise till he rises up in the morning from the east. There would be many stories now for the sun to tell upon his journey, if he had but a tongue to give them out.

III. THE NATURE OF THE STARS

THE stars now differ in their nature from one another. As to the ten stars of Gaburn, trembling takes hold of them, and fiery manes are put over their faces, to foretell a plague or a death of the people. Other stars there are that bring great heat or great cold or great mists upon the earth, others there are that run to encourage the dragons that blow lightnings on the world; others of them run to the end of fifty years and then ask their time for sleeping. To the end of seven years they sleep till they awake at the shout of the blessed angels, and the voices of the dragons of the valley. Others run through the six days and the six nights till the coming of the Sunday; at its beginning they begin their many kinds of music, and they fall alseep again till the coming again from heaven of God's Sunday, and with that they follow the same round.

THE CALL TO BRAN

ONE time Bran, son of Febal, was out by himself near his dun, and he heard music behind him. And it kept always after him, and at last he fell asleep with the sweetness of the sound. And when he awoke from his sleep he saw beside him a branch of silver, and it having white blossoms, and the whiteness of the silver was the same as the whiteness of the blossoms. And he brought the branch in his hand into the royal house, and when all his people were with him they saw a woman with strange clothing standing in the house. And she began to make a song for Bran, and all the people were looking at her and listening to her, and it is what she said: I bring a branch of the apple-tree from Emhain, from the far island around which are the shining horses of the Son of Lir. A delight of the eyes is the plain where the hosts hold their games: curragh racing against chariot in the Silver-White Plain to the south.

There are feet of white bronze under it, shining through life and time; a comely level land through the length of the world's age, and many blossoms falling on it.

There is an old tree there with blossoms, and birds calling from among them; every colour is shining there. Delight is common, and music in the Gentle Voiced Plain, in the Silver Cloud Plain to the south. There is nothing hard or rough, but sweet music striking on the ear; keening is not used, or treachery, in the tilled familiar land.

To be without grief, without sorrow, without death, without any sickness, without weakness; that is the sign of Emhain; it is not a common wonder that is.

There is nothing to liken its mists to, the sea washes the wave against the land; brightness falls from its hair.

Golden chariots in the Plain of the Sea, rising up to the sun with the tide; silver chariots and bronze chariots on the Plain of Sports.

It is a day of lasting weather, silver is dropping on the land; a pure white cliff on the edge of the sea, getting its warmth from the sun.

The host race over the Plain of Sports; it is beautiful and not weak their game is; death or the ebbing of the tide will not come to them in the Many-coloured Land.

There will come at sunrise a fair man, lighting up the level lands; he rides upon the plain that is beaten by the waves, he stirs the sea till it is like blood. An army will come over the clear sea, rowing to the stone that is in sight, that has a hundred sounds of music.

It sings a song to the army; it is not sad through the length of time; it increases music with hundreds singing together; they do not look for death or the ebb-tide.

THE ARMY OF THE SIDHE

LAEGAIRE, son of the king of Connacht, was out one day with the king his father near Loch na-n Ean, the Lake of Birds, and the men of Connacht with them, and they saw a man coming to them through the mist. Long golden-yellow hair he had, and at his belt a gold-hilted sword, and in his hand two five-barbed darts; a gold-rimmed shield on his back, a five-folded crimson cloak about his shoulders, and it is what he said:

The most beautiful of plains is the Plain of the Two Mists; it is not far from this; the men of its army in good order go out ahead of their beautiful king; they march among blue spears, white troops of fighters with curled hair.

They scatter the troops of their enemies, they destroy every country they make an attack on; they are beautiful in battle, a host with high looks, rushing, avenging.

It is no wonder they to have such strength every one of them is the son of a king and a queen; manes of hair they have of the colour of gold.

Their bodies smooth and comely; their eyes blue and far-seeing; their teeth bright like crystal within their thin red lips.

White shields they have in their hands, with patterns on them of white silver; blue shining swords, red horns set with gold. They are good at killing men in battle; good at song-making, good at chess-playing.

The most beautiful of plains is the Plain of the Two Mists; it is not far from this place.

CREDHE'S COMPLAINT AT THE BATTLE
OF THE WHITE STRAND

AND Credhe came to where her man was, and she keened him and cried over him, and she made this complaint:

The Harbour roars, O the harbour roars over the rushing race of the Headland of the Two Storms, the drowning of the hero of the Lake of the Two Dogs, that is what the waves are keening on the strand.

Sweet-voiced is the crane, O sweet-voiced is the crane in the marshes of the Ridge of the Two Strong Men; it is she cannot save her nestlings, the wild dog of two colours is taking her little ones.

Pitiful the cry, pitiful the cry the thrush is making in the Pleasant Ridge; sorrowful is the cry of the blackbird in Leiter Laeig.

Sorrowful the call, O sorrowful the call of the deer in the Ridge of Two Lights; the doe is lying dead in Druim Silenn, the mighty stag cries after her.

Sorrowful to me, O sorrowful to me the death of the hero that lay beside me; the son of the woman of the Wood of the Two Thickets, to be with a bunch of grass under his head.

Sore to me, O sore to me Cael to be a dead man beside me, the waves to have gone over his white body; it is his pleasantness that has put my wits astray.

A woeful shout, O a woeful shout the waves are making on the strand; they that took hold of comely Cael, a pity it is he went to meet them.

A woeful crash, O a woeful crash the waves are making on the strand to the north, breaking against the smooth rock, crying after Cael now he is gone.

A sorrowful fight, O a sorrowful fight, the sea is making with the strand to the north; my beauty is lessened; the end of my life is measured.

A song of grief, O a song of grief is made by the waves of Tulcha Leis; all I had is gone since this story came to me. Since the son of Crimthann is drowned I will love no one after him for ever; many a king fell by his hand; his shield never cried out in the battle.

After she had made that complaint Credhe laid herself down beside Cael and died for grief after him. And they were put in the one grave, and it was Caoilte raised the stone over them.

A SLEEPY SONG THAT GRANIA USED TO BE SINGING OVER DIARMUID THE TIME THEY WERE WANDERING AND HIDING FROM FINN

SLEEP a little, a little little, for there is nothing at all to fear, Diarmuid grandson of Duibhne; sleep here soundly, Diarmuid to whom I have given my love. It is I will keep watch for you, grandchild of shapely Duibhne; sleep a little, a blessing on you, beside the well of the strong field; my lamb from above the lake, from the banks of the strong streams.

Let your sleep be like the sleep in the North of fair comely Fionnchadh of Ess Ruadh, the time he took Slaine with bravery as we think, in spite of Failbhe of the Hard Head.

Let your sleep be like the sleep in the West of Aine daughter of Galian, the time she went on a journey in the night with Dubhthach from Dorinis, by the light of torches.

Let your sleep be like the sleep in the East of Deaghadh the proud, the brave fighter, the time he took Coincheann, daughter of Binn, in spite of fierce Decheall of Duibhreann.

O heart of the valour of the world to the west of Greece, my heart will go near to breaking if I do not see you every day. The parting of us two will be the parting of two children of the one house; it will be the parting of life from the body, Diarmuid.

HER SONG TO ROUSE HIM FROM SLEEP

THE stag to the east is not asleep, he does not stop from bellowing; though he is in the woods of the blackbirds, sleep is not in his mind; the hornless doe is not asleep, crying after her speckled fawn; she is going over the bushes, she does not sleep in her home.

The cuckoo is not asleep, the thrush is not asleep, the tops of the trees are a noisy place; the duck is not asleep, she is made ready for good swimming; the bog-lark is not asleep tonight on the high stormy bogs; the sound of her clear voice is sweet; she is not sleeping between the streams.

HER LAMENT FOR HIS DEATH

THEN when Grania was certain of Diarmuid's death she gave out a long very pitiful cry that was heard through the whole place, and her women and her people came to her, and asked what ailed her to give a cry like that. And she told them how Diarmuid had come to his death by the Boar of Beinn Gulbain in the hunt Finn had made. When her people heard that, they gave three great heavy cries in the same way, that were heard in the clouds and the waste places of the sky. And then Grania bade the five hundred that she had for household to go to Beinn Gulbain for the body of Diarmuid, and when they were bringing it back, she went out to meet them, and they put down the body of Diarmuid, and it is what she said: I am your wife, beautiful Diarmuid, the man I would do no hurt to; it is sorrowful I am after you to-night.

I am looking at the hawk and the hound my secret love used to be hunting with; she that loved the three, let her be put in the grave with Diarmuid.

Let us be glad to-night, let us make all welcome to-night, let us be open-handed to-night, since we are sitting by the body of a king.

And O Diarmuid, she said, it is a hard bed Finn has given you, to be lying on the stones and to be wet with the rain. Ochone! she said, your blue eyes to be without sight, you that were friendly and generous and pursuing. O love! O Diarmuid! it is a pity it is he sent you to your death.

You were a champion of the men of Ireland, their prop in the middle of the fight; you were the head of every battle; your ways were glad and pleasant.

It is sorrowful I am, without mirth, without light, but only sadness and grief and long dying; your harp used to be sweet to me, it wakened my heart to gladness. Now my courage is fallen down, I not to hear you but to be always remembering your ways. Och! my grief is going through me.

A thousand curses on the day when Grania gave you her love, that put Finn of the princes from his wits; it is a sorrowful story your death is to-day.

You were the man was best of the Fenians, beautiful Diarmuid, that women loved. It is dark your dwelling-place is under the sod, it is mournful and cold your bed is; it is pleasant your laugh was to-day; you were my happiness, Diarmuid.

THE PARTING OF GOLL AND HIS WIFE

AND when Goll knew Finn to be watching for his life he made no attempt to escape but stopped where he was, without food, without drink, and he blinded with the sand that was blowing into his eyes.

And his wife came to a rock where she could speak with him, and she called to him to come to her. "Come over to me," she said; "and it is a pity you to be blinded where you are, on the rocks of the waste sea, with no drink but the salt water, a man that was first in every fight. And come now to be sleeping beside me," she said; "and in place of the hard sea-water I will nourish you from my own breast, and it is I will do your healing," she said; "for it is seven years since you wedded with me, and from that night to this night I never got a hard word from you. And the gold of your hair is my desire for ever," she said, "and do not stop withering there like an herb in the winter-time, and my heart black with grief within me."

But Goll would not leave the spot where he was for all she could say. "It is best as it is," he said, "and I never took the advice of a woman east or west, and I never will take it. And O sweet-voiced queen," he said, "what ails you to be fretting after me; and remember now your silver and your gold, and your silks and stuffs, and remember the seven hounds I gave you at Cruadh Ceirrge, and every one of them without slackness till he has killed the deer. And do not be crying tears after me, queen with the white hands," he said; "but remember your constant lover, Aodh, the son of the best woman of the world, that came out from Spain asking for you, and that I fought at Corcar-an-Deirg. And go to him now," he said, "for it is bad when a woman is in want of a good man."

And he lay down on the rocks, and at the end of twelve days he died. And his wife keened him there, and made a great lamentation for her husband that had such a great name, and that was the second best of the Fenians of Ireland.

THE DEATH OF OSGAR

AND after a while, at noonday, they saw Finn coming towards them, and what was left of the Sun-banner raised on a spear-shaft. All of them saluted Finn then, but he made no answer, and he came up to the hill where Osgar was. And when Osgar saw him coming he saluted him, and he said, "I have got my desire in death, Finn of the sharp arms." And Finn said, "It is worse the way you were, my son, on the day of the battle of Ben Edair, when the wild geese could swim on your breast, and it was my hand that gave you healing." "There can no healing be done for me now for ever," said Osgar, "since the King of Ireland put the spear of seven spells through my body." And Finn said, "It is a pity it was not I myself fell in sunny scarce Gabhra, and you going east and west at the head of the Fenians." "And if it was yourself fell in the battle," said Osgar, "you would not hear me keening after you; for no man ever knew any heart in me," he said, "but a heart of twisted horn, and it covered with iron. But the howling of the dogs beside me," he said, "and the keening of the old fighting men and the crying of the women one after another, those are the things that are vexing me." And Finn said: "Child of my child, calf of my calf, white and slender, it is a pity the way you are. And my heart is starting like a deer," he said, "and I am weak after you and after the Fenians of Ireland. And misfortune has followed us," he said, "and farewell now to battles and to a great name, and farewell to taking tributes; for every good thing I ever had is gone from me now," he said. And when Osgar heard those words he stretched out his hands, and his eyelids closed. And Finn turned away from the rest, and he cried tears down; and he never shed a tear through the whole length of his lifetime but only for Osgar and for Bran.

OISIN'S VISION

I SAW the household of Finn; it was not the household of a soft race; I had a vision of that man yesterday.

I saw the household of the High King, he with the brown sweet-voiced son; I never saw a better man.

I saw the household of Finn; no one saw it as I saw it: I saw Finn with the sword, Mac an Luin. Och! it was sorrowful to see it.

I cannot tell out every harm that is on my head; free us from our trouble for ever; I have seen the household of Finn.

HIS PRAISE OF FINN

IT is a week from yesterday I last saw Finn; I never saw a braver man. A king of heavy blows; my law, my adviser, my sense and my wisdom, prince and poet, braver than kings, King of the Fenians, brave in all countries; golden salmon of the sea, clean hawk of the air, rightly taught, avoiding lies; strong in his doings, a right judge, ready in courage, a high messenger in bravery and in music.

His skin lime-white, his hair golden; ready to work, gentle to women; his great green vessels full of rough sharp wine. It is rich the king was, the head of his people.

Seven sides Finn's house had, and seven score shields on every side. Fifty fighting men he had about him having woollen cloaks; ten bright drinking-cups in his hall, ten blue vessels, ten golden horns.

It is a good household Finn had, without grudging, without lust, without vain boasting, without chattering, without any slur on any one of the Fenians. Finn never refused any man: he never put away any one that came to his house. If the brown leaves falling in the woods were gold, if the white waves were silver, Finn would have given away the whole of it.

OISIN AFTER THE FENIANS

Now my strength is gone from me, I that was adviser to the Fenians, my whole body is tired to-night, my hands, my feet, and my head; tired, tired, tired.

It is bad the way I am after Finn of the Fenians; since he is gone away, every good is behind me.

Without great people, without mannerly ways; it is sorrowful I am after our king that is gone.

I am a shaking tree, my leaves gone from me; an empty nut, a horse without a bridle; a people without a dwelling-place, I Oisin, son of Finn.

It is long the clouds are over me to-night! it is long last night was; although this day is long, yesterday was longer again to me; every day that comes is long to me.

That is not the way I used to be, without fighting, without battles, without learning feats, without young girls, without music, without harps, without bruising bones, without great deeds; without increase of learning, without generosity, without drinking at feasts, without courting, without hunting, the two trades I was used to; without going out to battle. Ochone! the want of them is sorrowful to me.

No hunting of deer or stag, it is not like that I would wish to be; no leashes for our hounds, no hounds; it is long the clouds are over me to-night!

Without rising up to do bravery as we were used, without playing as we had a mind; without swimming of our fighting men in the lake; it is long the clouds are over me to-night!

There is no one at all in the world the way I am; it is a pity the way I am; an old man dragging stones. It is long the clouds are over me to-night!

I am the last of the Fenians, great Oisin, son of Finn, listening to the voice of bells; it is long the clouds are over me to-night!

THE FORETELLING OF CATHBAD THE
DRUID AT DEIRDRE'S BIRTH

LET Deirdre be her name: harm will come through her. She will be fair, comely, bright-haired: heroes will fight for her, and kings go seeking for her.

O Deirdre, on whose account many shall weep, on whose account many women shall be envious, there will be trouble on Ulster for your sake, O fair daughter of Fedlimid.

Many will be jealous of your face, O flame of beauty; for your sake heroes shall go to exile. For your sake deeds of anger shall be done in Emain; there is harm in your face, for it will bring banishment and death on the sons of kings.

In your fate, O beautiful child, are wounds and ill-doings and shedding of blood.

You will have a little grave apart to yourself; you will be a tale of wonder for ever, Deirdre.

DEIRDRE'S LAMENT FOR THE SONS OF USNACH

As for Deirdre, she cried pitifully, wearily, and tore her fair hair, and she was talking of the sons of Usnach, and of Alban, and it is what she said:

A blessing eastward to Alban from me; good is the sight of her bays and valleys, pleasant was it to sit on the slopes of her hills, where the sons of Usnach used to be hunting.

One day, when the nobles of Alban were drinking with the sons of Usnach, Naoise gave a kiss secretly to the daughter of the lord of Duntreon. He sent her a frightened deer, wild, and a fawn at its foot; and he went to visit her coming home from the troops of Inverness. When myself heard that, my head filled full of jealousy; I put my boat on the waves, it was the same to me to live or to die. They followed me swimming, Ainnle and Ardan, that never said a lie; they turned me back again, two that would give battle to a hundred. Naoise gave me his true word, he swore three times with his arms as witness, he would never put vexation on me again, until he would go from me to the armies of the dead.

Och! if she knew to-night, Naoise to be under a covering of clay, it is she would cry her fill, and it is I would cry along with her!

After that Deirdre lay down by the grave, and they were digging earth from it, and she made this lament after the sons of Usnach:

Long is the day without the sons of Usnach; it was never wearisome to be in their company; sons of a king that entertained exiles; three lions of the Hill of the Cave.

Three darlings of the women of Britain; three hawks of Slieve Cuilenn; sons of a king served by valour, to whom warriors did obedience.

Three heroes not good at homage; their fall is a cause of sorrow; three sons of the sister of a king; three props of the army of Cuailgne.

The High King of Ulster, my first betrothed, I forsook for love of Naoise; short my life will be after him; I will make keening at their burial.

That I would live after Naoise let no one think on the earth; I will not go on living after Ainnle and after Ardan.

After them I myself will not live; three that would leap through the midst of battle; since my beloved is gone from me I will cry my fill over his grave.

O, young man, digging the new grave, do not make the grave narrow; I will be along with them in the grave, making lamentations and ochones!

Many the hardship I met with along with the three heroes; I suffered want of home, want of fire, it is myself that used not to be troubled.

Their three shields and their spears made a bed for me often. O, young man, put their three swords close over their grave!

Their three hounds, their three hawks, will be from this time without huntsmen; three aids of every battle; three pupils of Conall Cearnach.

The three leashes of those three hounds have brought a sigh from my heart; it is I had the care of them, the sight of them is a cause of grief.

I was never one day alone to the day of the making of this grave, though it is often that myself and yourselves were in loneliness.

My sight is gone from me with looking at the grave of Naoise; it is short till my life will leave me, and those who would have keened me do not live.

Since it is through me they were betrayed I will be tired out with sorrow; it is a pity I was not in the earth before the sons of Usnach were killed.

Sorrowful was my journey with Fergus, betraying me to the Red Branch; we were deceived all together with his sweet, flowery words. I left the delights of Ulster for the three heroes that were bravest; my life will not be long, I myself am alone after them.

I am Deirdre without gladness, and I at the end of my life; since it is grief to be without them, I myself will not be long after them!

EMER'S LAMENT FOR CUCHULAIN

AND Emer took the head of Cuchulain in her hands, and she washed it clean, and put a silk cloth about it, and she held it to her breast, and she began to cry heavily over it, and she made this complaint:

Och, head! Ochone, O head! you gave death to great heroes, to many hundreds; my head will lie in the same grave, the one stone will be made for both of us.

Och, hand! Ochone, hand, that was once gentle. It is often it was put under my head; it is dear that hand was to me.

Dear mouth! Ochone, kind mouth that was sweet-voiced telling stories; since the time love first came on your face, you never refused either weak or strong.

Dear the man, dear the man, that would kill the whole of a great army; dear his cold bright hair, and dear his bright cheeks!

Dear the king, dear the king, that never gave a refusal to any; thirty days it is to-night since my body lay beside your body.

Och, two spears! Ochone, two spears! Och, shield! Och, deadly sword! Let them be given to Conall of the battles; there was never any wage given the like of that.

I am glad, I am glad, Cuchulain of Muirthemne, I never brought red shame on your face, for any unfaithfulness against you.

Happy are they, happy are they, who will never hear the cuckoo again for ever, now that the Hound has died from us.

I am carried away like a branch on the stream; I will not bind up my hair to-day. From this day I have nothing to say that is better than Ochone! "And oh! my love," she said, "we were often in one another's company, and it was happy for us; for if the world had been searched from the rising of the sun to sunset, the like would never have been found in one place, of the Black Sainglain and the Grey of Macha, and Laeg the chariot-driver, and myself and Cuchulain. And it is breaking my heart is in my body, to be listening to the pity and the sorrowing of women and men, and the harsh crying of the young men of Ulster keening Cuchulain." And after that Emer bade Conall to make a wide, very deep grave for Cuchulain; and she laid herself down beside her gentle comrade, and she put her mouth to his mouth, and she said: "Love of my life, my friend, my sweetheart, my one choice of the men of the earth, many is the woman, wed or unwed, envied me till to-day; and now I will not stay living after you."

THE KILTARTAN HISTORY BOOK

THE FLOOD

AT the time of the Flood they were a hundred years making a bark. All the old logs of trees are in the bogs from that time, the time Ireland was drowned. The people got good warning. Noah kept in it the seed of each one, up to the birds that are in the air and every animal that is found in the world. Every blow that was struck on a nail by Noah was heard through the whole world. That was to give a warning. I often heard it came on the world to banish all out of it, and the seed was left, it to be formed by the Almighty God the way the people would flourish on again. After that again the whole world was burned, that the stones bursted and took fire from the heat of the sun, and the remains of the roots and the butts of bogdeal are to be found in the bogs. You to be cutting turf they will be rising. All the woods and valleys were burned with the heat of the sun, and even to stones would be split, and the people in their standing would be killed with the heat.

A GREAT MAN

MOSES was a great man and did great exploits; and no one knows the place he is buried, the same as Emmet. There was a search made for Emmet's grave and the place he was interred, and there was no one could discover it. It was Pharoah's daughter was out bathing and that found Moses that was put out on the river side, and that made him her heir. Pharoah was a great tyrant. He was near as bad as some of the Roman Emperors, such as Domitian. Moses stood up against him, he behaved well doing that. But he was cut off from a view of the Land of Promise because of his bad behaviour about water, doubting the mercy of God. When he was told to strike the rock once he struck it three times. And the people turned on him too, because they were always murmuring and he couldn't please them, just like the Irish that turned against Parnell.

THE JEWS

I HEARD many a thing of Moses but I don't know did he do the half of what they say he done. When God asked the Jews to be converted they wouldn't give in to him. God sent him to civilise them, as the disciples were sent after. The poorest Jew you would meet in any place, he would have money.

THE STRONGEST MAN

SAMSON was of the Irish race, all the world was Irish in those times, and he killed the Philistines and the eyes were picked out of him after. He was said to be the strongest, but I think myself Finn MacCumhail was stronger.

KING SOLOMON

SOLOMON was the richest man ever lived: look at his treasures and all he spent on the Temple, seven hundred millions of English money. And the Temple was burned after, in three days. It was Titus the Roman took Jerusalem, and he bade them all not to lay a hand on the Temple but someone set fire to it and it burned, and gold and silver were running out of it. All they found was the seven brass candlesticks. But Titus was a great man. He let no man or woman go downhearted from him; and he could keep three people in talk at the one time, and he writing on paper.

THE STRONG MEN

HERCULES was the strongest man. When he was a baby in the cradle his mother put a big serpent in the cradle with him to try his strength, and he twisted it and made an end of it. The stick he used to carry in his hand, it would make the earth shake the time he would put it to the ground. Samson was stronger again for what he had was Divine strength; but the strength Hercules had was human.

A REAL BEAUTY

HELEN that was a great beauty up to the age of fifty years. She must have been a real beauty to have been fine looking at that time. She looked in a body glass one time and saw the wrinkles coming on her face, and she went and hanged herself.

THE KING WITH A HORSE'S EARS

THERE was a King in Ireland in the old time and his hair grew very long, and as it would get too long he would get a barber to clip it, and after that he would put him to death, till hundreds were killed and there was no barber left. And the next time it was a doctor he got to clip it, and the doctor knew there must be some secret, and sure enough when he had it clipped he saw that the King had horse's ears. And the King did not kill him but put an oath upon him that he would tell no one what he had seen. So he took the oath, but it was hard on him to keep the secret and he went out to a crossroad where there was a willow tree and he spoke into the tree. Well, in those days there used to be a harper playing before the King. And when he went to play, one of the strings of the harp broke, and he went out to get something to mend it, and the best thing he saw for that was the willow tree at the crossroad, and he took a branch of it and mended the harp. And when he went down again to play before the King all it would play was "The King has got a horse's ears." So the King was very angry and he bade another harper to play, and he took the harp and in the same way all it would play was "The King has got a horse's ears." So after that he cut his hair short and tried to hide them no more.

THE OLD TIMES IN IRELAND

The first man ever lived in Ireland was Partholan, and he is buried and his greyhound along with him at some place in Kerry. The Nemidians came after that and stopped for a while and then they all died of some disease. And then the Firbolgs came, the best men that ever were in Ireland, and they had no law but love, and there was never such peace and plenty in Ireland. What religion had they? None at all. And there was a low sized race came that worked the land of Ireland a long time. They had their time like the others. Tommy Niland was sitting beside me one time the same as yourself, and the day warm as this day, and he said, "In the old times you could buy a cow for one and sixpence, and a horse for two shillings. And if you had lived in those days, Padraic, you'd have your cow and your horse." For there was a man in those times bought a cow for one and sixpence, and when he was driving her home he sat down by the roadside crying, for fear he had given too little. And the man that sold him as he was going home he sat down by the roadside crying, for fear he had taken too much. For the people were very innocent at that time and very kind. But Columcille laid it down in his prophecy that every generation would be getting smaller and more liary; and that was true enough. And in the old days if there was a pig killed, it would never be sent to the saltery but everyone that came in would get a bit of it. But now, a pig to be killed, the door of the house would be closed, and no one to get a bit of it at all. In the old times the people had no envy, and they would be writing down the stories and the songs for one another. But they are too venomous now to do that. And as to the people in the towns, they don't care for such things now, they are too corrupted with drink.

BALOR OF THE EVIL EYE

BALOR that lived up in Tory's Island could hear the wool growing on the sheep. And he could see three hundred miles. It was in a smith's forge he got his death; the smith's boy put a hot iron through him, calling to him of a sudden to look around.

THE FIANNA OF IRELAND

THE Fianna were very strong in those days, and six or seven feet high. They would go to all countries in curraghs that were as strong as steamers; to Spain they went in their curraghs. They went across from that hill of Burren at one time, and the sea opened to let them pass. But they had no religion, and every man made a God of himself. There are no men like them now. The Connemara men are the best, but even with them, if there was a crowd of them together and you to throw a stick over their heads it would hardly hit one; they are mostly all the one height and no one a few inches taller than another. They were all strong men in those times, and one time Finn and his men went over to Granagh to fight the men there, and it was the time of the harvest and what they fought with was sheaves, and everyone that got a blow of a sheaf got his death. Giants they were; and they lived longer than people do now, three or four hundred years. Weren't they great people! Forty-one fires in one house. It is dogs they used to have, and to live by hunting and killing meat. Maybe they ate nuts sometimes, for there were some people such as Saints used to go into the wilderness and to live on nuts and herbs they would gather, when they laid their mind to it. But ever since people are getting smaller and smaller, and will till they come to the end. But they are wittier and more crafty than they were in the old days; for the Giants were innocent, though they were so strong.

FINN MACCUMHAIL, THEIR LEADER

Finn MacCumhail was a great man. Every hair of his head had the full strength of a man in it. He was a very nice man, with fair hair hanging down his back like a woman; a grand man he was. When he would chew his little finger he would know all things, and he understood enchantments as well. It is the way he got his wisdom, he was driven away by the natives, and he took service with a great king. And there was a prophecy there would be a very big salmon caught some day in the river, and so there was, and it was given to Finn to cook, but he was to be beheaded if he let any spot come on it. And he saw a bulge in the skin, and he put his finger on it to put it down. And from that time, whenever he would put his finger to his mouth knowledge would come to him.

HIS WISDOM

HE could do as much and understand as much as a child of a twelvemonth old, and no other man had that much knowledge. What can a child of a twelvemonth do that we cannot do? Did you never see a child, the way it is busy about the house and doing little things, and no one knowing how it does them. The mother herself can't understand what the child is doing, and that is the time she takes the most pride in him. Goll MacMorna was the strongest, but Finn had the most wisdom.

THEIR STRENGTH

The Connacht men make a boast that Goll was the strongest but I think myself Osgar was the best, because it was in fair fight he won. But the time Goll had the fight with Dearg Mor, that lasted through three days, Dearg Mor used to be brought away by the women every night, and there was music and dancing and he got no rest, but Goll used to have his full sleep. And I don't think that was very fair dealing.

GRANIA

FINN had more wisdom than all the men of the world, but he wasn't wise enough to put a bar on Grania. It was huts with big stones Grania made, that are called cromlechs now. She and Diarmuid made them when they went away into the wilderness. Many would tell you Grania slept under the cromlechs, but I don't believe that, and she a king's daughter. And I don't believe she was handsome either. If she was, why would she have run away? Grania was Finn's wife, and she went away with Diarmuid. She left him after and came back to Finn, but they never got on well together. She left him again and was for twenty years with Diarmuid, and Finn took her back. It was a great delusion Finn taking her back that time. The third time he would not take her back, it was within two years of his death, and he said he had had enough of bad living. As they were passing a stream the water splashed on Grania and she said, "Diarmuid has never come so near to me as that." It was with enchantment Finn coaxed her, and with enchantment he killed Diarmuid too.

CONAN

ONE time the King of the Danes sent a messenger to Finn and bade him come there and marry his daughter. But it was to make a trap for him he did that, the way he would kill him. But when the messenger came he stood for a while and said nothing, and Conan that was son of a mermaid hit him with his fist when he didn't speak after coming in. And Finn said, "You are teaching manners to another and you have no manners yourself." They were all vexed with Conan because he was so cross and so contrary and they couldn't teach him manners; and they said he should not come with them to Lochlann. Conan was angry then and he went to Finn and said he should go. And Finn said, "Can I have no quiet at all with you always fighting? And I will not bring you with us," he said. And Conan said, "That you may be seven hundred times worse this time next year, if you are the king, and if you did get your knowledge from a blind salmon. And that you may never be cross till you meet with your death," he said. That was a great curse to put upon him. Then Usheen gave Conan a place in his boat, but Osgar drove him out of it again. Conan gave them great abuse then and reproached Usheen with his mother being a deer, for Conan always had a stone in his pocket. And then he went and cut the sails and the masts of the other ships that were ready for the Fianna. Some of them set on him then to make an end of him, but he ran from them. Finn called to him to come back, for his brothers would not let him be harmed. But Conan said, "There is no use in having brothers if you haven't got a good pair of feet to run with as well."

MANNANAN, SON OF THE SEA

THEN Conan went to Mannanan son of Lir, that had all sorts of enchantments, and asked for his help to follow them over the sea. "And I will make a little boat for myself," he said, "and I will twist it in and out with wicker-work." "You need not go to that trouble," said Mannanan, "for I will lend you my own boat." It was for the sake of the Fianna he that was the King of the Sidhe did that, for the fairies were very friendly to the Fianna at that time. And the boats had fairy music with them and they going over to Lochlann. One time the Fianna were fighting in some place, and they were driving away the enemy's cattle, and they were attacked, and Mannanan, son of Lir, came to help them, and he said, "I will do the fighting and you can drive away the cattle." "Do not," they said, "but we will fight and you can drive away the cattle." "Then I will do both," he said. "I will fight and I will drive away the cattle." And he did that. The King of Denmark's daughter? It is only to trap them he sent his message to Finn. How do I know if he had one at all?

CONAN'S ARMS

THERE was an old man near this, beside the sea, had a song that gave the coats of arms of the Fianna, and Conan's was a briar. That was because he was always drawing troubles and quarrels between them. That cairn you see beyond on the big mountain to the west of Burren is said by the Connacht men to be where Conan is buried. They say there was a stone found there one time that had on it this writing, "Conan the swiftfooted, the barefooted." He was not so strong as Goll MacMorna, that would break down a gate with a stone, but he was a good runner, he would come up with a deer. He was not so nice as the others. He was some way cross.

USHEEN IN TIR-NAN-OGE

USHEEN was the last of the Fianna and the greatest of them. It's he was brought away to Tir-Nan-Oge, that place where you'd stop for a thousand years and be as young as the first day you went. Out hunting they were, and there was a deer came before them very often, and they would follow it with the hounds, and it would always make for the sea, and there was a rock a little way out in the water, and it would leap on to that, and they wouldn't follow it. So one day they were going to hunt, they put Usheen out on the rock first, the way he could catch a hold of the deer and be there before it. So they found it and followed it, and when it jumped on to the rock Usheen got a hold of it. But it went down into the sea and brought him with it to some enchanted place underground that was called Tir-Nan-Oge, and there he stopped a very long time, but he thought it was only a few days he was in it. It is in that direction, to the west he was brought, and it was to the Clare coast he came back. And in that place you wouldn't feel the time passing, and he saw the beauty of heaven and kept his youth there a thousand years. It is a fine place, and everything that is good is in it. And if anyone is sent there with a message he will want to stop in it, and twenty years of it will seem to him like one half-hour. But as to where Tir-Nan-Oge is, it is in every place, all about us.

HIS RETURN TO IRELAND

WELL, when he thought he had been a twelvemonth there, he began to wish to see the strong men again, his brothers; and he asked whoever was in authority in that place to give him a horse and to let him go. And they told him his brothers were all dead, but he wouldn't believe it. So they gave him a horse, but they bade him not to get off it or to touch the ground while he would be away; and they put him back in his own country. And when he went back to his old place, there was nothing left of the houses but broken walls, and they covered with moss; and all his friends and brothers were dead, with the length of time that had passed. And where his own home used to be he saw the stone trough standing that used to be full of water, and where they used to be putting their hands in and washing themselves. And when he saw it he had such a wish and such a feeling for it that he forgot what he was told and got off the horse. And in a minute it was as if all the years came on him, and he was lying there on the ground, a very old man and all his strength gone.

USHEEN AND PATRICK

IT was before the Flood those strong men lived here, Finn and Usheen and the others; and they lived longer than people do now, three or four hundred years. Usheen lived the longest of all, because of all those years he was away in a trance. He was saved after that by Saint Patrick. But all the others are said to be in hell because they cared nothing about God. For if one of us has a field of oats or of barley ripening in the sun we'll say, "Thanks be to God." But if they had a field of oats or of barley ripening, they'd be thankful to one another or to themselves, for they thought themselves to be as much as God. Did he have much trouble to convert him? Not at all; he was as blind as that floor.

THE ARGUMENTS

IT was after Usheen fell from his horse, Saint Patrick began to instruct and to convert him. And he asked where all his companions were, and Goll the champion of Ireland. And it is what Saint Patrick said that God had them all shut up in hell with the devil. And Usheen said, "If I could see them I would draw them out of that, and the devil with them and his whole forge." And Saint Patrick told him about Adam and Eve and how they were turned out and lost for eating the forbidden fruit, an apple he called it. And Usheen said, "Although God has all my friends shut up in hell, if I knew fruit was so scarce with him, and he to think so much of it, I'd have sent him seven cartloads of it." It was very decent of Usheen to say that; he always had a very decent name for those sort of things. And Usheen said another thing to Patrick. He said, "Don't the blackbird and the thrush whistle very well, and don't they make their nests very nice, and they never got any instruction or teaching from God?" And what Saint Patrick answered to that I don't know. It was not long after that Saint Patrick got him converted, and as soon as he converted him he was in such a hurry not to lose a minute but to baptize him at once, that he struck down his spear on his foot without seeing it, and pinned him by the instep to the ground. And when he saw a stream of blood coming from the instep he said, "Why did you make no sign when the spear struck you?" And Usheen said, "I thought it was part of the rite of baptism. And I wouldn't begrudge a little drop of blood to God Almighty." He died soon after that and was saved, because he showed such patience. But all his friends are in hell; but when they lived angels used to come sometimes to see them and to talk with them; they were so nice and so respectable.

SAINT PATRICK

THERE were many great saints in Ireland, but Saint Patrick was the bush among them all. He used to be travelling and blessing all before him. He was about seventy years when God bade him come to Ireland, and he didn't like to be put out of his way, being old, and he said he would not come. So then God said if he would not come he would give him a bad next door neighbour that would be fighting and quarrelling and slandering him. So when he heard that, he said it would be as good to go to Ireland.

THE DRUIDS' CANDLE

SAINT Patrick came one night to a farmer's house, and there was a great candle shining in some place near, and three or four of the farmer's sons had got their death through it, for every one that would see it would get his death. It was some evil thing that put it there, witchcraft that the Druids used to be doing at that time the way the Freemasons do it in England to this day. They do that, and they have a way of knowing each other if they would meet in a crowd. But Saint Patrick went to where the candle was, and it did him no harm and he put it out, and it was never lighted again in Ireland.

CUCHULAIN AND AOIFE'S SON

I WILL tell you now about Cuchulain that was the greatest man that came in Ireland after the time of the Fianna. He beat the King of Connacht in three battles, and the King of Connacht had the help of the English called in. Cuchulain went one time to get learning of fighting from a witch in some place that is far away. She had a vessel in the water, and when any man came wanting her daughter in marriage she would say he must walk through the vessel first. And when he did that he would fall in the water, up to the waist, and all the flesh would go from him and nothing be left but the bones. But when Cuchulain came, she said if he would marry herself he need not go in the vessel at all. So he married her and he lived with her a year all but three months, and at the end of that time he said he must go back to Ireland. "Oh, why would you go from me?" she said. "I must go see my armies," said Cuchulain. "And when the child is born," he said, "if it is a son, give it my own name; but if it is a girl you may do with it what you like." So he went away, but she thought to herself she would vex his heart yet. And the son was born and she reared him till he was nineteen years, and then she sent him to Ireland. And she bade him tell his name to no one but to go there and to fight and to put down the best man in Ireland. So he went to land in Ireland, and twelve men came down to stand against him, and he put them all down and tied them together and left them there. And then he went up and asked to fight with the best man in Ireland. And Cuchulain came out and he said, "Tell me what your name is?" And the young man said, "I did not come out to tell it to one or to two. But if I told it to anyone in the whole world," he said, "it is I would soonest tell it to your pale face." For he felt in his heart that it was his father was before him. So they went fighting then, and it was with spears they used to fight at that time. And the son would throw them fair and easy every time but Cuchulain would throw them hard and wicked at him. And one of Cuchulain's spears went through his body at the last. And when he was lying on the ground near his death Cuchulain asked him who was he. And he told him he was his own son. "And did you not see me throw the spears fair and easy?" he said; "and you threw them hard and wicked at me."

MAEVE OF CONNACHT

As to Queen Maeve she was very handsome, and used the hazel stick, that her enemies could not stand before her. But she grew very disagreeable after that; you wouldn't like to hear all that is said of her. Better not to be talking about it; who knows how much of it is true? Let it be between the book and the reader.

GOBAN, THE BUILDER

THE Goban was the master of sixteen trades. There was no beating him; he had got the gift. He went one time to Quin Abbey when it was building, looking for a job, and the men were going to their dinner, and he had poor clothes, and they began to jibe at him, and the foreman said, "Make now a cat-and-nine-tails while we are at our dinner, if you are any good." And he took the chisel and cut it in the rough in the stone, a cat with nine tails coming from it, and there it was complete when they came out from their dinner. There was no beating him. He learned no trade, but he was master of sixteen. That is the way, a man that has the gift will get more out of his own brain than another will get through learning. There is many a man without learning will get the better of a college-bred man, and will have better words too. Those that make inventions in these days have the gift, such a man now as Edison, with all he has got out of electricity.

A WITTY WIFE

THE Goban Saor was a mason and a smith, and he could do all things, and he was very witty. He was going from home one time and he said to the wife, "If it is a daughter you have this time I'll kill you when I come back"; for up to that time he had no sons, but only daughters. And it was a daughter she had; but a neigh-bouring woman had a son at the same time, and they made an exchange to save the life of the Goban's wife. But when the boy began to grow up he had no wit, and the Goban knew by that he was no son of his. That is the reason he wanted a witty wife for him. So there came a girl to the house one day, and the Goban Saor bade her look round at all that was in the room, and he said, "Do you think a couple could get a living out of this?" "They could not," she said. So he said she wouldn't do, and he sent her away. Another girl came another day, and he bade her take notice of all that was in the house, and he said, "Do you think could a couple knock a living out of this?" "They could if they stopped in it," she said. So he said that girl would do. Then he asked her could she bring a sheepskin to the market and bring back the price of it, and the skin itself as well. She said she could, and she went to the market, and there she pulled off the wool and sold it and brought back the price and the skin as well. Then he asked could she go to the market and not be dressed or undressed. And she went having only one shoe and one stocking on her, so she was neither dressed or undressed. Then he sent her to walk neither on the road or off the road, and she walked on the path beside it. So he said then she would do as a wife for his son.

AN ADVICE SHE GAVE

ONE time some great king or lord sent for the Goban to build a *caislean* for him, and the son's wife said to him before he went, "Be always great with the women of the house, and always have a comrade among them." So when the Goban went there he coaxed one of the women the same as if he was not married. And when the castle was near built, the woman told him the lord was going to play him a trick, and to kill him or shut him up when he had the castle made, the way he would not build one for any other lord that was as good. And as she said, the lord came and bade the Goban to make a cat and two-tails, for no one could make that but himself, and it was meaning to kill him on it he was. And the Goban said he would do that when he had finished the castle, but he could not finish it without some tool he had left at home. And they must send the lord's son for it—for he said it would not be given to any other one. So the son was sent, and the Goban sent a message to the daughter-in-law that the tool he was wanting was called "When you open it shut it." And she was surprised, for there was no such tool in the house; but she guessed by the message what she had to do, and there was a big chest in the house and she set it open. "Come now," she said to the young man, "look in the chest and find it for yourself." And when he looked in she gave him a push forward, and in he went, and she shut the lid on him. She wrote a letter to the lord then, saying he would not get his son back till he had sent her own two men, and they were sent back to her.

SHORTENING THE ROAD

HIMSELF and his son were walking the road together one day, and the Goban said to the son, "Shorten the road for me." So the son began to walk fast, thinking that would do it, but the Goban sent him back home when he didn't understand what to do. The next day they were walking again, and the Goban said again to shorten the road for him, and this time he began to run, and the Goban sent him home again. When he went in and told the wife he was sent home the second time, she began to think, and she said, "When he bids you shorten the road, it is that he wants you to be telling him stories." For that is what the Goban meant, but it took the daughter-in-law to understand it. And it is what I was saying to that other woman, that if one of ourselves was making a journey, if we had another along with us, it would not seem to be one half as long as if we would be alone. And if this is so with us, it is much more with a stranger, and so I went up the hill with you to shorten the road, telling you that story.

THE GOBAN'S SECRET

THE Goban and his son were seven years building the castle, and they never said a word all that time. And at the end of seven years the son was at the top, and he said, "I hear a cow lowing." And the Goban said then, "Make all strong below you, for the work is done," and they went home. The Goban never told the secret of his building, and when he was on the bed dying they wanted to get it from him, and they went in and said, "Clare-galway Castle is after falling in the night." And the Goban said, "How can that be when I put a stone in and a stone out and a stone across." So then they knew the way he built so well.

THE SCOTCH ROGUE

ONE time he was on the road going to the town, and there was a Scotch rogue on the road that was always trying what could he pick off others, and he saw the Connemara man—that was the Goban—had a nice cravat, and he thought he would get a hold of that. So he began talking with him, and he was boasting of all the money he had, and the Goban said whatever it was he had three times as much as it, and he with only thirty pounds in the world. And the Scotch rogue thought he would get some of it from him, and he said he would go to a house in the town, and he gave him some food and some drink there, and the Goban said he would do the same for him on the morrow. So then the Goban went out to three houses, and in each of them he left ten pounds of his thirty pounds, and he told the people in every house what they had to do, and that when he would strike the table with his hat three times they would bring out the money. So then he asked the Scotch rogue into the first house, and ordered every sort of food and drink, ten pounds worth in all. And when they had used all they could of it, he struck with his hat on the table, and the man of the house brought out the ten pounds, and the Goban said, "Keep that to pay what I owe you." The second day he did the same thing in another house. And in the third house they went to he ordered ten pounds worth of food and drink in the same way. And when the time came to pay, he struck the table with the hat, and there was the money in the hand of the man of the house before them. "That's a good little caubeen," said the Scotch rogue, "when striking it on the table makes all the money appear." "It is a wishing hat," said the Goban; "anything I wish for I can get as long as I have that." "Would you sell it?" said the Scotch rogue. "I would not," said the Goban. "I have another at home, but I wouldn't sell one or the other." "You may as well sell it, so long as you have another at home," said the Scotch rogue. "What will you give for it?" says the Goban. "Well you give three hundred pounds for it?" "I will give that," says the Scotch rogue, "when it will bring me all the wealth I wish for." So he went out and brought the three hundred pound, and gave it to the Goban, and he got the caubeen and went away with it, and it not worth three halfpence. There was no beating the Goban. Wherever he got it, he had got the gift.

THE DANES

FINN was the last of the Giants, the tall, strong men. It was after that the Lochlanachs came to the country, that were a small race and dark and carried the bag. But they were more crafty than the Giants, and they used to be humbugging them. One time they got a sack and filled it with sand and gave it to one of the Fianna to put on his back to try him. But he lifted it up and all he said was,

"It is grain sowed in February it is." They were surely small men, or how could they live in those little rooms and passages in the raths? I'd have to stoop myself down when I'd go into them. They had the whole country once, and they used to make beer out of the tops of the heath the same way the bees draw honey out of it. A raven to hover near the house is bad, keeping quiet on the wing. It was a raven one of the Danish leaders had that used to go here and there, and come back to his shoulder and be whispering newses into his ear. The Italians give in greatly to birds, but religion tells us not to believe in them. Weasels were cats to the Danes, and many's the good battle I saw between a weasel and a good rat. They are the best of fishermen catching fish in the sea, for they are enchanted. But there's nothing on the face of the globe so awful as a cat.

WHAT THEY LEFT AFTER THEM

THERE were some digging in a marshy place and they found barrels that were buried by the Danes, eight or ten of them. And they opened them and put in a hand, and there was nothing at the top but tallow, so they sold them to one Damer, a chandler. That is the way he got rich and had a room full of gold. It was a tailor that worked for him asked for a sight of the gold. "What good is that to you?" said Damer. "It is all you get of it yourself," said the tailor; and Damer gave him a hatful of the gold. And there was a ship full of pipes found not many years ago that was left by the Danes. They had pipes in those days, but what they put in them is not known, for it was Sir Walter Raleigh brought tobacco to Ireland, and it was the poet Spenser first planted a leaf of it in his garden. But some say tobacco was in the world at all times, and there's no one but would be the better for it, only a delicate man that would use too much. And there's women in the world use as much as ourselves, and they with their pipe in their gob. But as to tea, before it was in the world people didn't die so sudden as what they do.

NEWS OF THE DANES

THERE was a man one time set out from Ireland to go to America or some place, a common man looking for work he was. And something happened to the ship on the way and they had to put to land to mend it. And in the country where they landed he saw a forth and he went into it, and there he saw the smallest people he ever saw, and they were the Danes that went out of Ireland, and it was they had foxes for dogs and weasels were their cats. And when there is a marriage among the Danes they put down the land they have in Ireland with whatever else they have, for they expect to come back and to own the country again some day. But whether they will or not, I don't know.

THE WISPS

THE reason of the wisps and the fires on Saint John's Eve is that one time long ago the Danes came and took the country and conquered it, and they put a soldier to mind every house through the whole country. And at last the people made up their mind that on one night they would kill its soldiers. So they did as they said, and there wasn't one left, and that is why they light the wisps ever since. It was Brian Boroihme was the first to light them. There was not much of an army left to the Danes that time, for he made a great scatter of them. A great man he was, and his own son was as good, that is Murrough. It was the wife brought him to his end, Gormleith. She was for war, and he was all for peace. And he got to be very pious, too pious, and old, and she got tired of that.

THE BATTLE OF CLONTARF

CLONTARF was on the head of a game of chess. The generals of the Danes were beaten at it, and they were vexed; and Cennedigh was killed on a hill near Fermoy. He put the Holy Gospels in his breast as a protection, but he was struck through them with a reeking dagger. It was Brodar, that the Brodericks are descended from, that put a dagger through Brian's heart, and he attending to his prayers. What the Danes left in Ireland were hens and weasels. And when the cock crows in the morning the country people will always say "It is for Denmark they are crowing. Crowing they are to be back in Denmark."

THE ENGLISH

IT WAS a long time after that, the Pope encouraged King Henry to take Ireland. It was for a protection he did it, Henry being of his own religion, and he fearing the Druids or the Danes might invade Ireland.

THE QUEEN OF BREFFNY

DERVORGILLA was a red-haired woman, and it was she put the great curse on Ireland, bringing in the English through Mac-Murrough, that she went to from O'Rourke. It was to Henry the Second MacMurrough went, and he sent Strongbow, and they stopped in Ireland ever since. But who knows but another race might be worse, such as the Spaniards that were scattered along the whole coast of Connacht at the time of the Armada. And the laws are good enough. I heard it said the English will be dug out of their graves one day for the sake of their law. As to Dervorgilla, she was not brought away by force, she went to MacMurrough herself. For there are men in the world that have a coaxing way, and sometimes women are weak.

KING HENRY VIII

HENRY THE EIGHTH was crying and roaring and leaping out of the bed for three days and nights before his death. And he died cursing his children, and he that had eight millions when he came to the Throne, coining leather money at the end.

ELIZABETH

QUEEN ELIZABETH was awful. She was a very lustful woman. Beyond everything she was. When she came to the turn she dyed her hair red, and whatever man she had to do with, she sent him to the block in the morning, that he would be able to tell nothing. She had an awful temper. She would throw a knife from the table at the waiting ladies, and if anything vexed her she would maybe work upon the floor. A thousand dresses she left after her. Very superstitious she was. Sure after her death they found a card, the ace of hearts, nailed to her chair under the seat. She thought she would never die while she had it there. And she bought a bracelet from an old woman out in Wales that was over a hundred years. It was superstition made her do that, and they found it after her death tied about her neck.

HER DEATH

IT was a town called Calais broke her heart and brought her to her death the same as the Boer War did with Queen Victoria, and she lay chained on the floor three days and three nights. The Archbishop was trying to urge her to eat, but she said, "You would not ask me to do it if you knew the way I am," for nobody could see the chains. After her death they waked her for six days in Whitehall, and there were six ladies sitting beside the body every night. Three coffins were about it, the one nearest the body of lead, and then a wooden one, and a leaden one on the outside. And every night there came from them a great bellow. And the last night there came a bellow that broke the three coffins open, and tore the velvet, and there came out a stench that killed the most of the ladies and a million of the people of London with the plague. Queen Victoria was more honourable than that. It would be hard to beat Queen Elizabeth.

CAROLAN'S SONG

CAROLAN, that could play the fiddle and the harp, used to be going about with Cahil-a-Corba, that was a tambourine man. But they got tired of one another and parted, and Carolan went to the house of the King of Mayo, and he stopped there, and the King asked him to stop for his lifetime. There came a grand visitor one time, and when he heard Carolan singing and playing and his fine pleasant talk, he asked him to go with him on a visit to Dublin. So Carolan went, and he promised the King of Mayo he would come back at the end of a month. But when he was at the gentleman's house he liked it so well that he stopped a year with him, and it wasn't till the Christmas he came back to Mayo. And when he got there the doors were shut, and the King was at his dinner, and Queen Mary and the three daughters, and he could see them through the windows. But when the King saw him he said he would not let him in. He was vexed with him and angry, he had broken his promise and his oath. So Carolan began to give out a song he had made about the King of Mayo and all his family, and he brought Queen Mary into it and the three daughters. Then the Queen asked leave of the King to bring him in, because he made so good a song, but the King would not give in to it. Then Carolan began to draw down the King of Mayo's father and his grandfather into the song. And Queen Mary asked again for forgiveness for him, and the King gave it that time because of the song that had in it the old times, and the old generations went through him. But as to Cahil-a-Corba, he went to another gentleman's house and he stopped too long in it and was driven out. But he came back, having changed his form, that the gentleman did not know him, and he let him in again, and then he was forgiven.

THE TRACE OF CROMWELL

I'LL tell you now about the trace of Cromwell. There was a young lady was married to a gentleman, and she died with her first baby, and she was brought away into a forth by the fairies, the good people, as I suppose. She used to be sitting on the side of it combing her hair, and three times her husband saw her there, but he had not the courage to go and to bring her away. But there was a man of the name of Howley living near the forth, and he went out with his gun one day and he saw her beside the forth, and he brought her away to his house, and a young baby sprang between them at the end of a year. One day the husband was out shooting and he came in upon Howley's land, and when young Howley heard the shooting he rose up and went out and he bade the gentleman to stop, for this was his land. So he stopped, and he said he was weary and thirsty, and he asked could he rest in the house. So young Howley said as long as he asked pardon he had leave to use what he liked. So he came in the house and he sat at the table, and he put his two eyes through the young lady. "If I didn't see her dead and buried," he said, "I'd say that to be my own wife." "Oh!" said she, "so I am your wife, and you are badly worthy of me, and you have the worst courage ever I knew, that you would not come and bring me away out of the forth as young Howley had the courage to bring me," she said. So then he asked young Howley would he give him back his wife. "I will give her," he said, "but you never will get the child." So the child was reared, and when he was grown he went travelling up to Dublin. And he was at a hunt, and he lost the top of his boot, and he went into a shoemaker's shop and he gave him half a sovereign for nothing but to put the tip on the boot, for he saw he was poor and had a big family. And more than that, when he was going away he took out three sovereigns and gave them to the shoemaker, and he looked at one of the little chaps, and he said, "That one will be in command of the whole of England." "Oh, that cannot be," said the shoemaker, "where I am poor and have not the means to do anything for him." "It will be as I tell you," said he, "and write me out now a docket," he said, "that if ever that youngster will come to command Ireland, he will give me a free leg." So the docket was made out, and he brought it away with him. And sure enough, the shoemakers son listed, and was put at the head of soldiers, and got the command of England, and came with his soldiers to put down Ireland. And Howley saw them coming and he tied his handkerchief to the top of his stick, and when Cromwell saw that, he halted the army, "For there is some poor man in distress," he said. Then Howley showed him the docket his father had written. "I will do some good thing for you on account of that," said Cromwell; "and go now to the top of that high cliff," he said, "and I'll give as much land as you can see from it." And so he did give it to him. It was no wonder Howley to have known the shoemaker's son would be in command and all would happen him, because of his mother that got knowledge in the years she was in the forth. That is the trace of Cromwell. I heard it at a wake, and I would believe it, and if I had time to put my mind to it, and if I was not on the road from Loughrea to Ballyvaughan, I could give you the foundations of it better.

CROMWELL'S LAW

I'LL tell you about Cromwell and the White Friars. There was a White Friar at that time was known to have knowledge, and Cromwell sent word to him to come see him. It was of a Saturday he did that, of an Easter Saturday, but the Friar never came. On the Sunday Cromwell sent for him again, and he didn't come. And on the Monday he sent for him the third time, and he did come. "Why is it you did not come to me when I sent before?" said Cromwell. "I'll tell you that," said the White Friar. "I didn't come on Saturday," he said, "because your passion was on you. And I didn't come on the Sunday," he said, "because your passion was not gone down enough, and I thought you would not give me my steps. But I came to-day," he said, "because your passion is cool." When Cromwell heard his answer, "That is true," he said, "and tell me how long my law will last in Ireland." "It will last," says the White Friar, "till yesterday will come (that was Easter Sunday) the same day as our Lady Day." Cromwell was satisfied then, and he gave him a free leg, and he went away. And so that law did last till now, and it's well it did, for without that law in the country you wouldn't be safe walking the road having so much as the price of a pint of porter in your pocket.

CROMWELL IN CONNACHT

CROMWELL cleared the road before him. If any great man stood against him he would pull down his castle the same as he pulled down that castle of your own, Ballinamantane, that is down the road. He never got more than two hours sleep or three, or at the most four, but starting up fearing his life would be peppered.

There was a word he sounded out to the Catholics, "To hell or Connacht," and the reason he did that was that Connacht was burned bare, and he that thought to pass the winter there would get no lodging at all. Himself and his men travelled it, and they never met with anything that had human breath put in it by God till they came to Breffny, and they saw smoke from a chimney, and they surrounded the house and went into it. And what they saw was a skeleton over the fire roasting, and the people of the house picking flesh off it with the bits of a hook. And when they saw that, they left them there. It was a Clare man that burned Connacht so bare; he was worse than Cromwell, and he made a great slaughter in the house of God at Clonmel. The people have it against his family yet, and against the whole County of Clare. O'Donnell from the North came down by the seaside burning everything before him from mansions to the poorest cabin. He came from Ballyvaughan to Kiltartan and passed a night there, but because it was the Sabbath he did nothing, but went on to Tuam Graney. Those neighbours of your own beyond were in with Oliver Cromwell in the days gone by, and he saved them when he ran through the whole country. It is the way that happened, he was stopping in the house and the lady liked him well, and when he was going away he said, "If it is a boy let you call him Oliver." And so when the time came it is Oliver he was called. So he left them all they had, and they the only ones he did leave a share to in the Province of Connacht. That is the story from the old time, and if there was not something in it, why would he tell the lady to call him Oliver?

A WORSE THAN CROMWELL

CROMWELL was very bad but the drink is worse. For a good many that Cromwell killed should go to heaven, but those that are drunk never see heaven. And as to drink, a man that takes the first glass is as quiet and as merry as a pet lamb; and after the second glass he is as knacky as a monkey; and after the third glass he is as ready for battle as a lion; and after the fourth glass he is like a swine as he is. "I am thirsty" "*Tha Tort Orm,*" that was one of our Lord's seven words on the Cross, where he was dry. And a man far off would have given him drink; but there was a drunkard at the foot of the Cross, and he prevented him.

THE CROMWELLIAN SETTLEMENT

PRENDERGAST was a great writer. He wrote the Cromwellian settlement. It is he would have put down Harry Froude better than the man that took in hand to do it, that was Father Tom Burke. For Prendergast got to the Castle, he had a great job getting leave to do that, and he found the letters that were thick and piled with dust, and made out the truth from them. He was a long time doing that; two or three months and he could hear the trumpets of the guard every day. And after that he defied anyone to say he wrote down any lie.

A POEM MADE IN IRISH IN
CROMWELL'S TIME

THE Gael are flayed and stripped entirely; a grave is made ready for every one of them; or they make no delay but take their pass and cross the ocean, giving their word to stop away to the time of their death from Ireland.

Though the strength of the Gall is beyond our strength, and though they got luck and fortune among us, they will not get the sway by the dint of their twists, but the anger of God will rain down upon them. O! Father of miracles, we have leave to pray to you. Give back their rights to the Gael of Ireland!

ANOTHER POEM WRITTEN IN IRISH,
AT THE END OF CROMWELL'S WAR

IT is to all the Gael of Inisfail I am telling out this sharp story that has left me full of sorrow. My grief for our brave fighting men, the weight of their defeat and their need.

Their roots have been cut away and perished along with their means and their great name. Not the length of a foot of their lands left to them, nor so much as the makings of a bed; but only leave to bring away their life to Spain.

There will be coming after them to take their place, after destroying themselves, their civility and their cities, the fat-legged mockers with their packs and plates and brass and pewter; with their English chat.

PATRICK SARSFIELD

SARSFIELD was a great general the time he turned the shoes on his horse. The English it was were pursuing him, and he got off and changed the shoes the way when they saw the tracks they would think he went another road. That was a great plan. He got to Limerick then, and he killed thousands of the English. He was a great general.

THE STUARTS

As to the Stuarts, there are no songs about them and no praises in the West, whatever there may be in the South. Why would there, and they running away and leaving the country the way they did? And what good did they ever do it? James the Second was a coward. Why didn't he go into the thick of the battle like the Prince of Orange? He stopped on a hill three miles away, and rode off to Dublin, bringing the best of his troops with him. There was a lady walking in the street at Dublin when he got there, and he told her the battle was lost, and she said, "Faith you made good haste; you made no delay on the road." So he said no more after that. The people liked James well enough before he ran; they didn't like him after that.

ANOTHER STORY

SEUMUS Salach, Dirty James, it is he brought all down. At the time of the battle there was one of his men said, "I have my eye cocked, and all the nations will be done away with," and he pointing his cannon. "Oh!" said James, "Don't make a widow of my daughter." If he didn't say that, the English would have been beat. It was a very poor thing for him to do. I used to hear them singing "The White Cockade" through the country—"King James was beaten and all his well-wishers; my grief, my boy, that went with them!" But I don't think the people had ever much opinion of the Stuarts; but in those days they were all prone to versify. But the Famine did away with all that. Sure King James ran all the way from the Boyne to Dublin after the battle. There was a verse made about him. "It was the coming of King James that struck down Ireland, With his one shoe Irish and his one shoe English, He that wouldn't strike a blow and that wouldn't make a peace, he has left trouble for ever on the Gael."

THE BISHOP OF DERRY

THERE will never be tranquility in Ireland. Look now at the North that is making ready to fight, the same as at the time of William of Orange. The Bishop of Derry came out to the battle of the Boyne and took his place in the ranks and he was the first to be killed in the battle. "What brought him into it?" said William when they told that to him. There was a statue put up to him and it stood through the years, through wind and water, till the day the King's assent was given to Catholic emancipation; and on that day the sword fell from his hand. But as to the Belfast men, the Prince of Orange could get no good of them, but to hand them over to Ginkel.

THE BALL AT ATHLONE

SEVEN or eight nations were in the battle of Aughrim—Scotch and Scot; Irish and Dutch and Danes, Hessians, Hanoverians, Brandenburgians—they came with William of Orange. And they were in it in '98. William of Orange was a soldier down to his boots. St. Ruth was too careless. And he put a curse upon the Irish; he asked why was he brought out of France for to lead such a race. But he was too slow himself. He had the surrounding gentry invited to a ball just before the battle of Aughrim, and when his messenger came to warn him the English were crossing the Shannon in three troops, all he did was to say, "Tell them St. Ruth is here." He thought that his name would frighten them.

THE BATTLE OF AUGHRIM

THAT was a great slaughter at Aughrim. St. Ruth wanted to do all himself, he being a foreigner. He gave no plan of the battle to Sarsfield, but a written command to stop where he was, and Sarsfield knew no more than yourself or myself in the evening before it happened. It was Colonel Merell's wife bade him not go to the battle, where she knew it would go bad with him through a dream. But he said that meant that he would be crowned, and he went out and was killed. That is what the poem says:

> "If Caesar listened to Calpurnia's dream
> He had not been by Pompey's statue slain."

All great men gave attention to dreams, though the Church is against them now. It is written in Scripture that Joseph gave attention to his dream. But Colonel Merell did not, and so he

went to his death. Aughrim would have been won if it wasn't for
the drink. There was too much of it given to the Irish soldiers that
day—drink and spies and traitors. The English never won a battle
in Ireland in fair fight, but getting spies and setting the people
against one another. I saw where Aughrim was fought and I turned
aside from the road to see the tree where St. Ruth was killed. The
half of it is gone like snuff. That was spies too, a Colonel's daughter
that told the English in what place St. Ruth would be washing
himself at six o'clock in the morning. And it was there he was shot
by one O'Donnell, an Englishman. He shot him from six miles off.
The Danes were dancing in the raths around Aughrim the night
after the battle. Their ancestors were driven out of Ireland before;
and they were glad when they saw those that had put them out
put out themselves, and every one of them skivered.

A LAMENT MADE IN IRISH FOR SARSFIELD

O PATRICK SARSFIELD, health be to you, since you went to France
and your camps were loosened; making your sighs along with the
King, and you left poor Ireland and the Gael defeated—Och
ochone! O Patrick Sarsfield, it is a man with God you are; and
blessed is the earth you ever walked on. The blessing of the bright
sun and the moon upon you, since you took the day from the hands
of King William—Och ochone! O Patrick Sarsfield, the prayer
of every person with you; my own prayer and the prayer of the
Son of Mary with you, since you took the narrow ford going
through Biorra, and since at Cuilenn O'Cuarac you won Limerick
—Och ochone! I will go up on the mountain alone; and I will
come hither from it again. It is there I saw the camp of the Gael,
the poor troop thinned, not keeping with one another—Och
ochone! My five hundred healths to you, halls of Limerick, and
to the beautiful troop was in our company; it is bonfires we used
to have and playing cards, and the word of God was often with us
—Och ochone! There were many soldiers glad and happy that
were going the way through seven weeks; but now they are
stretched down in Aughrim—Och ochone! They put the first
breaking on us at the Bridge of the Boyne; the second breaking
on the Bridge of Slaney: the third breaking in Aughrim of O'Kelly;
and O sweet Ireland my five hundred healths to you—Och ochone!
O'Kelly has manuring for his land that is not sand or dung, but
ready soldiers doing bravery with pikes, that were left in Aughrim
stretched in ridges—Och ochone! Who is that beyond on the hill,
Beinn Edair? I a poor soldier with King James. I was last year in
arms and in dress, but this year I am asking alms—Och ochone!

THE STORY OF IRELAND TO THE
DEFEAT AT AUGHRIM AS THE LITTLE
BUSH TOLD THE POET RAFTERY IN IRISH

IT is the wind from the west that has perished me from top to
root. It is a long time I am stopping in this place; it is many a
story I can give news of. The time the eight were saved and the
thousands were drowned, Noah and his clan and his mother, it
was on the side of Croagh Patrick that Partholan was kept living
by the will of the Graces. It is the Ridge of the wild Boar was the
name of this place; there was nothing in it only wood and wilderness; wild dogs and badgers making their leaps, till the time the
Firblogs came to Ireland. Hunting on hills and hunting on the
mountain, great the strength of the whole of them together; till
the people without grace came against them, the Tuatha de Danaan
from the land of Egypt. I, the Bush of Athlinn, saw all this; and
saw the two armies coming together. And the finishing of the case
and the end of the story; and the Firbolg banished by a race without humanity. Gaedelus came next, of the race of Milesius, a
royal prince of the true blood of the Gael; his sons, MacCuill,
MacCeacht, MacGreine, with their sharp bright swords, divided
Ireland. There was a man of them was not satisfied; then began
robbery, wrong and treachery. Lands and provinces going through
one another, till Cormac son of Art put his hand to Ireland. It
is he drew together the Fianna of Ireland; Goll son of Morna with
his polished sword; Caoilte and Osgar, Diarmuid O'Duibne that
raised enchantments; Finn; the man of knowledge, the choice
of the fighting men. It is under myself the strong men made their
sport; playing and drinking every day and every night. Their
shields, their helmets and their sharp-edged swords on the table
under me along with their full cups. Hunting on the hills, on the
bogs and mountains; running after the badgers and the hornless
does; till as swift as a hound, destruction came on them, because
they would never give in to God. Conochar came to the Crown
after that; and the good champions trained to bravery. The Sons
of Usnach that put Scotland under rent: but the three were lost
on the head of Deirdre. Cuchulain of the feats, the Hound that
broke every gap: and Curoi that was lost through the beauty of
Blanad; Fergus MacRoy, and Conall Cearnach—not one of
them was sanctified but only Conochar. Not one was of the
Saints till the coming of Patrick; a blessed Apostle that travelled
to Ireland. He quenched the Candle of the Rock by his rod. He
put seven hundred churches together. Another throng came

after that story; the Lochlannachs that put trouble on Ireland. Turgesius their leader tearing and destroying; a foreign soldier put in every house, in dread would the secret thought of any two come together. Until Brian Boroimhe took pity on Ireland and the kingdom started up all together; put watchers to kill the Danes and to light the wisps, on the Eve of Saint John in every corner of Ireland. Early in the morning of the Friday of the Crucifixion, between the Ford of Hurdles and the harbour on Beinn Edair, the Lochlannachs were running like a fox before the hounds. But Brian and his children, the strong men, were lost. Another hundred years after this story, the King of Leinster took, unless lies were put out, the wife from O'Rourke that left trouble on the Gael, and brought the English for the first time to Ireland. A message was sent out and a horn blowing, till many hundreds were gathered together; Strongbow, the lord over them and leader, till they brought under their sway the Province of Leinster. Three hundred years, and put more to it, till the crooked Prince was born in England; and Martin Luther, bad were his habits, who denied the Pope and the Holy Sacrament. One thousand and five hundred as may be read; nine and eight to be put along with it, since Christ came down in the body of a man; till Henry began the Reformation. Turned his back on God and denied his wife; married his own daughter as wife and comrade; wasn't it a crooked law that one had, to put his wife and daughter to death together. Then Queen Mary, the hound of the Gael; the civil, mannerly, comely maiden. She pulled up bushes and trees and branches. if it wasn't that she died she'd have pulled up the root. Elizabeth came to the Crown after that; who never took a mate and never fasted from a man. She turned her back to the yoke of the clergy, till she put to the rout the Church of the Gael. The next to come after her was James, the man that was the worst for law and for manners. He gave obedience to the law of Strafford; putting his chain upon bog and mountain. And no worse was the father than the son Charles; laying his heavy scourge on Ireland. But when God and man had a mind for the news, he lost his head through the five of Trumps. Maguire and MacMahon raised a hand for Ireland. The heads were struck off the two of them in London. Owen Roe came after that in the story, the gay, mannerly, civil horseman, that knocked a side-leap out of the Cromwellians. The time there was trouble in the month of harvest, in Aughrim, on the day that follows the Sunday, it left grief on many of the sons of the Gael, without a word at all of the defeat at the Boyne. The curse of God upon James of the Dirt, that gave his daughter to William for a woman of a wife. He made the Irish English and the English Irish, when he put through one another the wheat and the barley. The English were feasting at Cillin-O-Guaire, till the time Sarsfield came, the generous-hearted; he sent down into the Shannon their pride and their arms. And raised the siege of Limerick that very morning. Let ye not be without courage from this time out. God is stronger than the Cromwellians. That is what Raftery put down about Ireland; Himself and the little Bush together.

QUEEN ANNE

THE Georges were fair; they left all to the Government; but Anne was very bad and a tyrant. She tyrannised over the Irish. She died brokenhearted with all the bad things that were going on about her. For Queen Anne was very wicked. Oh! she was the wickedest woman that ever lived! No one can tell how wicked she was! (I think this old woman, lying in her Workhouse bed, had in her mind Aine, a Queen in the fairy kingdom. So in an old ballad, a call to a girl to join the invisible host, she is told:—

"There is not a forth from this to the North
But we'll dance all around it and sing merrily;
And the lads of Queen Anne shall be at your command,
And they shall all stand in great dread of thee."

In like manner some of the legends of Dean Swift have evidently come from some far earlier tradition of the Danes; the "ea" being often given the sound of "a" in Ireland.)

THE DEAN OF ST. PATRICK'S

DEAN Swift was a great man; very sharp-tongued he was, and fond of women terribly. Himself and his man Jack went riding to some place and they went for shelter into a public house. There was a fire on the hearth and there were two men sitting beside it and they made no offer to move aside, where the Dean and Jack wore very simple clothes, knee breeches as the gentlemen used to do. So the Dean says to Jack, "Did you put up the horses?" "I did," says Jack. "What did you give them for a feed?" says the Dean. "I gave them a feed of oysters," says Jack. So when the two men heard that they went out for to look at the great wonder, the horses to be eating oysters. And when they came in, the Dean and Jack had their two places taken by the fire. The Dean was eating his dinner one time and he gave Jack but the bone with very little left on it. "It is the sweetest bit that is next the bone," says he. Well, a while after they were on the road, and he bade Jack to tie up his horse where he'd have a feed of grass. So Jack brought him to a big stone and tied his head to it. "Why did you tie him in that place?" says the Dean. "Sure you told me yourself," says Jack, "the sweetest of the grass is next the stone!" Some eggs Jack brought him one time, in his hand, just as you might be bringing them to a man out on a bog. "Let you put a plate under everything you will bring from this out," says the Dean. So the next morning when Jack brought up his boots, he had put a plate under them. The Dean sent Jack for a woman one night, and it was a black woman Jack brought up to the hotel, and the Dean never saw her till morning, and when he did he thought it was the devil. He sacked Jack that time. "What were you sacked for?" says Jack's mother. "It is that he sent me for a pullet and I brought back a hen," says Jack. "That's no great fault," says the mother and she went to the Dean and said he had a right to take Jack back again, and so he did.

A SON OF THE DEAN

THERE was a son of Dean Swift was a great rider, and the Dean made him a bet of two hundred pounds that he would not leap over the drop at the edge of the cliffs of Moher, where there is a wall close to the brink. But the son made a leap sideways over the wall, that was standing sideways the same as that press, and so he was over the drop in the leap, but he landed again on the ground. He won the two hundred pounds doing that. There was another son of the Dean that was called Fireball, and that used to put his own son standing out in the front of the house and an egg on his head, and he would fire his gun and put the two halves of the egg to different sides. Hadn't the son a great nerve to stand and let him do that? But Fireball said he would shoot him if he did not.

THE WAR WITH AMERICA

THE Americans stood out in the harbour of Boston and boycotted all before them. It was with the help of the French they beat the English. They were so weak they were afraid to sign the Independence, thinking the English might turn back, and it was an Irishman was the first to sign it. O'Carolan I think his name was.

THE VOLUNTEERS

A HUNDRED thousand Volunteers there were. That was in 1792, the time England was at war with America, and the Volunteers were armed to keep off invasion. And when they got arms in their hands they asked for freedom. And the English came back then from America after being beat by General Washington, and they wanted to put down the Volunteers, so they promised them freedom, to make them lay down their arms. And no sooner had they laid down their arms than the English broke their word, just the same as they did at Limerick the time of Sarsfield and of the Treaty. Broke their word within three days, and the ink it was written with hardly dry.

IN GRATTAN'S TIME

THERE are Volunteers drilling in Gort now (1914) the same as in Grattan's time in 1793. The English were at war with America at that time, and if the Volunteers held to their arms, Ireland would be free. But the English made them disarm, being so witty and so keen, and what could they do then? Look at Carson the other day. They wanted him to do the same thing, but he said No, he'd hold to his arms.

'NINETY-EIGHT

In the year '98 there were the Yeomanry that were the worst of all. The time Father Murphy was killed there was one of them greased his boots in his heart. There was one of them was called Micky the Devil in Irish; he never went out without the pitchcap and the triangle, and any rebel he would meet he would put gunpowder in his hair and set a light to it. The North Cork Militia were the worst; there are places in Ireland where you would not get a drink of water if they knew you came from Cork. And it was the very same, the North Cork, that went on their own free will to the Boer war, volunteered, asked to go that is. They had the same sting in them always. A great many of them were left dead in that war, and a great many better men than themselves. There was one battle in that war there was no quarter given, the same as Aughrim; and the English would kill the wounded that would be left upon the field of battle. There is no Christianity in war.

DENIS BROWNE

There is a tree near Denis Browne's house that used to be used for hanging men in the time of '98, he being a great man in that time, and High Sheriff of Mayo, and it is likely the gentlemen were afeared, and that there was bad work at nights. But one night Denis Browne was lying in his bed, and the Lord put it in his mind that there might be false information given against some that were innocent. So he went out and he brought out one of his horses into the lawn before the house, and he shot it dead and left it there. In the morning one of the butlers came up to him and said, "Did you see that one of your horses was shot in the night?" "How would I see that?" says he, "and I not rose up or dressed?" So when he went out they showed him the horse, and he bade the men to bury it, and it wasn't two hours after before two of them came to him. "We can tell you who it was shot the horse," they said. "It was such a one and such a one in the village, that were often heard to speak bad of you. And besides that," they said, "we saw them shooting it ourselves." So the two that gave that false witness were the last two Denis Browne ever hung. He rose out of it after, and washed his hands of it all. And his big house is turned into a convent, and the tree is growing there yet. It is in the time of '98 that happened, a hundred years ago.

THE UNION

As to the Union, it was bought with titles. Look at the Binghams and the rest, they went to bed nothing, and rose up lords in the morning. The day it was passed Lady Castlereagh was in the House of Parliament, and she turned three colours, and she said to her husband, "You have passed your treaty, but you have sold your country." He went and cut his throat after that. And it is what I heard from the old people, there was no priest in Ireland but voted for it, the way they would get better rights, for it was only among poor persons they were going at that time. And it was but at the time of the Parliament leaving College Green they began to wear the Soutane that they wear now. Up to that it was a bodycoat they wore and knee-breeches. It was their vote sent the Parliament to England, and when there is a row between them or that the people are vexed with the priest, you will hear them saying in the house in Irish, "Bad luck on them, it was they brought misfortune to Ireland." They wore the Soutane ever since that time.

ROBERT EMMET

The Government had people bribed to swear against Robert Emmet, and the same men said after, they never saw him till he was in the dock. He might have got away but for his attention to that woman. She went away after with a sea captain. There are some say she gave information. Curran's daughter she was. But I don't know. He made one request, his letters that she wrote to him in the gaol not to be meddled with, but the Government opened them and took the presents she sent in them, and whatever was best of them they kept for themselves. He made the greatest speech from the dock ever was made, and Lord Norbury on the bench, checking and clogging him all the time. Ten hours he was in the dock, and they gave him no more than one dish of water all that time; and they executed him in a hurry, saying it was an attack they feared on the prison. There is no one knows where is his grave.

EMMET'S DRESS

It was a pity to hang so fine a man. I was looking at his picture a while ago, and his dress, very nice, knee breeches and a collar turned over, they dressed very nice in those days. But now you'll see a man having a thing stiff the same as a washboard in front of him, and one button in it, and you wouldn't know has he a soutane under it or anything at all. It is likely the linen Emmet was wearing was made at home, for I remember the days when every house had flax sowed in the garden. There was a man going to be hanged in Galway one time and his wife went to see him the night before, and all she said was, "Where will I sow the flax this year?" He was vexed at that and he said, "Is that all you are come to say to me?" "Is it that you are in a sulk because you are going to to be hanged in the morning?" says the wife. That was all she said.

CURRAN'S DAUGHTER

Robert Emmet would have been let off if he would give up his cause but he would not, because he was a gentleman. And the night he was taken he could have made his escape. There was a boat waiting and a ship out to sea to bring him away into France. But he would not go without he could go say good-bye to Curran's daughter, and what good was there in that? Couldn't he have written a letter to her upon paper with a pen? But he would go

see her himself; he was a gentleman and a grand man, and like all
the great men of that time he was a strong Protestant. It is likely
she was downhearted for a long while after losing him.

CURRAN

As to Curran he was a Judge, and there was a boy brought before
him for stealing gooseberries, and he gave him three months in
gaol. "And now," says he, "it is likely you will put your curses on
gooseberries." "I will, and on *Currans*," says the boy. Wasn't he
a smart boy to think of that? There was another smart lad was
brought into Court as a witness, and before he was let take the
oath they asked him did he know where he would go if he broke it.
"I do," says he. "Where's that?" says the Judge. "To the same
place where the lawyers go," says he. For there was a man went
to Heaven one time and he asked was there any lawyer there, and
there was not one to be found.

O'CONNELL'S BIRTH

O'Connell was a grand man, and whatever cause he took in hand,
it was as good as won. But what wonder? He was the gift of God.
His father was a rich man, and one day he was out walking he took
notice of a house that was being built. Well, a week later he passed
by the same place, and he saw the walls of the house were no
higher than before. So he asked the reason, and he was told it
was a priest that was building it, and he hadn't the money to go
on with. So a few days after he went to the priest's house and he
asked was that true, and the priest said it was. "Would you pay
back the money to the man that would lend it to you?" says
O'Connell. "I would," says the priest. So with that O'Connell
gave him the money that was wanting—£50—for it was a very
grand house. Well, after some time the priest came to O'Connell's
house, and he found only the wife at home, so says he, "I have
some money that himself lent me." But he had never told the
wife of what he had done, so she knew nothing about it, and says
she, "Don't be troubling yourself about it, he'll bestow it on you."
"Well," says the priest, "I'll go away now and I'll come back
again." So when O'Connell came, the wife told him all that had
happened, and how a priest had come saying he owed him money,
and how she had said he would bestow it on him. "Well," says
O'Connell, "if you said I would bestow it, I will bestow it." And

so he did. Then the priest said, "Have you any children?" "Ne'er a child," said O'Connell. "Well you will have one," said he. And that day nine months their young son was born. So what wonder if he was inspired, being, as he was, the gift of God.

THE TINKER

O'Connell was a great man. I never saw him, but I heard of his name. One time I saw his picture in a paper, where they were giving out meal, where Mrs. Gaynor's is, and I kissed the picture of him. They were laughing at me for doing that, but I had heard of his good name. There was some poor man, a tinker, asked help of him one time in Dublin, and he said, "I will put you in a place where you will get some good thing." So he brought him to a lodging in a very grand house and put him in it. And in the morning he began to make saucepans, and he was making them there, and the shopkeeper that owned the house was mad at him to be doing that, and making saucepans in so grand a house, and he wanted to get him out of it, and he gave him a good sum of money to go out. He went back and told that to O'Connell, and O'Connell said, "Didn't I tell you I would put you in the way to get some good thing?"

A PRESENT

There was a gentleman sent him a present one time, and he bade a little lad to bring it to him. Shut up in a box it was, and he bade the boy to give it to himself, and not to open the box. So the little lad brought it to O'Connell to give it to him. "Let you open it yourself," says O'Connell. So he opened it, and whatever was in it blew up and made an end of the boy, and it would have been the same with O'Connell if he had opened it.

HIS STRATEGY

O'Connell was a grand man; the best within the walls of the world. He never led anyone astray. Did you hear that one time he turned the shoes on his horses? There were bad members following him. I cannot say who they were, for I will not tell what I don't know. He got a smith to turn the shoes, and when they came upon his track, he went east and they went west. Parnell was no bad man, but Dan O'Connell's name went up higher in praises.

THE MAN WHO WAS GOING TO BE HANGED

I saw O'Connell in Galway one time, and I couldn't get anear him. All the nations of the world were gathered there to see him. There were a great many he hung and a great many he got off from death, the dear man. He went into a town one time, and into a hotel, and he asked for his dinner. And he had a frieze dress, for he was very simple, and always a clerk along with him. And when the dinner was served to him, "Is there no one here," says he, "to sit along with me; for it is seldom I ever dined without company." "If you think myself good enough to sit with you," says the man of the hotel, "I will do it." So the two of them sat to the dinner together, and O'Connell asked was there any news in the town. "There is," says the hotel man, "there is a man to be hung tomorrow." "Oh, my!" says O'Connell, "what was it he did to deserve that?" "Himself and another that had been out fowling," says he, "and they came in here and they began to dispute, and the one of them killed the other, and he will be hung to-morrow." "He will not," says O'Connell. "I tell you he will," says the other, "for the Judge is come to give the sentence." Well, O'Connell kept to it that he would not, and they made a bet, and the hotel man bet all he had on the man being hung. In the morning O'Connell was in no hurry out of bed, and when the two of them walked into the Court, the Judge was after giving the sentence, and the man was to be hung. "*Maisead*," says the judge when he saw O'Connell, "I wish you had been here a half-an-hour ago, where there is a man going to be hung." "He is not," says O'Connell. "He is," says the judge. "If he is," says O'Connell, "that one will never let anyone go living out of his hotel, and he making money out of the hanging." "What do you mean saying that?" says the judge. Then O'Connell took the instrument out of his pocket where it was written down all the hotelkeeper had put on the hanging. And when the judge saw that, he set the man free, and he was not hanged.

THE CUP OF THE SASSANACH

He was over in England one time, and he was brought to a party, and tea was made ready and cups. And as they were sitting at the table, a servant girl that was in it, and that was Irish, came to O'Connell and she said, "Do you understand Irish, O'Connell?" It is in Irish she said that, and he answered her in Irish, "I understand it." "Have a care," says she, "for there is in your cup what would poison the whole nation!" "If that is true, girl, you will get a good fortune," said he. It was in Irish they said all that, and the people that were in it had no ears. Then O'Connell quenched the candle, and he changed his cup for the cup of the man that was next him. And it was not long till the man fell dead. They were always trying to kill O'Connell, because he was a good man. The Sassanach it was were against him. Terrible wicked they were, and God save us, I believe they are every bit as wicked yet!

A GRAND MAN

Is that O'Connell's picture up there? He is a grand man. Did I ever tell you of the way he saved the man that stole a horse? He came to a town and there was a man to be tried for stealing a horse, and the wife came to O'Connell asking him to get him off. And he said to the wife, "There is but one way to get him off, and that is for yourself to join with the man that is against him, in swearing he did steal the horse." So in Court the woman got up and said it was true he did steal it. Then O'Connell said to the Judge, "It's easy to see this woman and the man that accused him are great with one another, and they had a plan made up to hang the husband and to banish him out of the world." And the Judge thought the same thing; so the husband was let off. Wasn't O'Connell a good man to think of that?"

IN THE WORKHOUSE

"It was in London they tried to poison him," says an old woman in the Workhouse. "I saw the hotel where that was done." "What was the name of it?" said another old woman. "The Prince and Eagles. It is a good thing he had the Irish that time." "It is a good thing he had the Irish girl," says the first old woman. "He went through the whole world serving Ireland. All for Ireland he was. He got great cheering that day he was in Gort."

THE THOUSAND FISHERS

O'Connell came to Galway one time, and he sent for all the trades to come out with the sign of their trade in their hand, and he would see which was the best. And there came ten hundred fishers, having all white flannel clothes and black hats and white scarves about them, and he gave the sway to them. It wasn't a year after that, the half of them were lost, going through the fogs at Newfoundland, where they went for a better way of living.

WHAT THE OLD WOMEN SAW

THE greatest thing I ever saw was O'Connell driving through Gort, very plain, and an oiled cap on him, and having only one horse; and there was no house in Gort without his picture in it. O'Connell rode up Crow Lane and to Church Street on a single horse, and he stopped there and took a view of Gort. I saw O'Connell after he left Gort going on the road to Kinvara, and seven horses in the coach—they could not get in the eighth. He stopped, and he was talking to Hickman that was with me. Shiel was in the coach along with him.

A SONG MADE IN IRISH BY RAFTERY
FOR THE CLARE ELECTION IN 1829 WHEN
DANIEL O'CONNELL CAME OUT ON TOP

THE Turks and the Greeks are striking at one another, and thousands will be lost on this side and that. The English and the French will be taking aim at one another, and Ireland will be lighted with the edge of swords. I pray to Jesus who suffered on a Friday that I may never go to death till the time comes when every side of them will be hitting at one another and till we'll get our pleasure of the Orangemen. If all that is written about Ireland is true, it is long till our asking will be brought to a head, "Emancipation" to be brought under seal; leave for the Gael to be as high as the Gall. It is said by Shiel and Lawless, by O'Connell and O'Gorman, that we'll get satisfaction without much delay. The Thistle will wither and the bloom fall from it; the Lion will be on the ground and no strength in him. For it is long it was given out that the bright day would come, when the Harp would play to us in the year of the Nine. Guns and fires and bonfires will be with us to-morrow, and it is time. Since O'Connell got the victory over the enemy the blossoms will open and there will be fruit upon the trees. In the county of Clare there are nobles and high princes shaking the hand and making sport. But we will be rocking under the quart till we'll drink the health of all the men from Aran as far as Inchiquin.

O'CONNELL'S HAT

O'CONNELL wore his hat in the English House of Commons, what no man but the King can do. He wore it for three days because he had a sore head, and at the end of that they bade him put it off, and he said he would not, where he had worn it three days.

THE CHANGE HE MADE

O'CONNELL was a great Councillor. At that time if there was a Catholic, no matter how high or great or learned he was, he could not get a place. But if a Protestant came that was a blockhead and ignorant, the place would be open to him. There was a revolution rising because of that, and O'Connell brought it into the House of Commons and got it changed. He was the greatest man ever was in Ireland. He was a very clever lawyer; he would win every case, he would put it so strong and clear and clever, If there were fifteen lawyers against him—five and ten—he would win it against them all, whether the case was bad or good.

THE MAN HE BROUGHT TO JUSTICE

CORLY, that burned his house in Burren, was very bad, and it was O'Connell brought him to the gallows. The only case O'Connell lost was against the Macnamaras, and he told them he would be even with them, and so when Corly, that was a friend of theirs, was brought up he kept his word. There was no doubt about him burning the house, it was to implicate the Hynes he did it, to lay it on them. There was a girl used to go out milking at daybreak, and she awoke, and the moon was shining, and she thought it was day, and got up and looked out, and she saw him doing it.

THE BINDING

O'CONNELL was a great man, wide big arms he had. It was he left us the cheap tea; to cheapen it he did, that was at that time a shilling for one bare ounce. His heart is in Rome and his body in Glasnevin. A lovely man, he would put you on your guard; he was for the country, he was all for Ireland.

HIS MONUMENT

THERE is a nice monument put up to O'Connell in Ennis, in a corner it is of the middle of a street, and himself high up on it, holding a book. It was a poor shoemaker set that going. I saw him in Gort one time, a coat of O'Connell's he had that he chanced in some place. Only for him there would be no monument; it was he gathered money for it, and there was none would refuse him.

A PRAISE MADE FOR DANIEL O'CONNELL
BY OLD WOMEN AND THEY BEGGING
AT THE DOOR

DAN O'CONNELL was the best man in the world, and a great man surely; and there could not be better than what O'Connell was. It was from him I took the pledge and I a child, and kept it ever after. He would give it to little lads and children, but not to any aged person. Pilot trousers he had and a pilot coat, and a grey and white waistcoat. O'Connell was all for the poor. See what he did at Saint Patrick Island—he cast out every bad thing and every whole thing, to England and to America and to every part. He fought it well for every whole body. A splendid monument there is to him in Ennis, and his fine top coat upon him. A lovely man; you'd think he was alive and all, and he having his hat in his hand. Everyone kneels down on the steps of it and says a few prayers and walks away. It is as high as that tree below. If he was in Ireland now the pension would go someway right. He was the best and the best to everyone; he got great sway in the town of Gort, and in every other place. I suppose he has the same talk always; he is able to do for us now as well as ever he was; surely his mercy and goodness are in the town of Gort. He did good in the world while he was alive; he was a great man surely; there couldn't be better in this world I believe, or in the next world; there couldn't be better all over the world. He used to go through all nations and to make a fight for the poor; he gave them room to live, and used to fight for them too. There is no doubt at all he did help them, he was well able to do it.

RICHARD SHIEL

As to Shiel, he was small, dressed very neat, with knee-breeches and a full vest and a long-skirted coat. He had a long nose, and was not much to look at till he began to speak, and then you'd see genius coming out from him. His voice was shrill, and that spoiled his speech sometimes, when he would get excited, and would raise it at the end. But O'Connell's voice you would hear a mile off, and it sounded as if it was coming through honey.

THE TITHE WAR

AND the Tithes, the tenth of the land that St. Patrick and his Bishops had settled for their own use, it was to Protestants it was given. And there would have been a revolution out of that, but it was done away with, and it is the landlord has to pay it now. The Pope has a great power that is beyond all. There is one day and one minute in the year he has that power if it pleases him to use it. At that minute it runs through all the world, and every priest goes on his knees and the Pope himself is on his knees, and that request cannot be refused, because they are the grand jury of the world before God. A man was talking to me about the burying of the Tithes; up on the top of the Devil's Bit it was, and if you looked around you could see nothing but the police. Then the boys came riding up, and white rods in their hands, and they dug a grave, and the Tithes, some image of them, was buried. It was a wrong thing for one religion to be paying for the board of the clergy of another religion.

THE FIGHT AT CARRICKSHOCK

THE Tithe War, that was the time of the fight at Carrickshock. A narrow passage that was in it, and the people were holding it against the police that came with the Proctor. There was a Captain defending the Proctor that had been through the Battle of Waterloo, and it was the Proctor they fired at, but the Captain fell dead, and fourteen police were killed with him. But the people were beat after, and were brought into court for the trial, and the counsel for the Crown was against them, Dougherty. They were tried in batches, and every batch was condemned, Dougherty speaking out the case against them. But O'Connell, that was at that time at Cork Assizes, heard of it, and he came, and when he got to the door the pony that brought him dropped dead. He came in and took refreshment—bread and milk—the same as I am after taking now, and he looked up and he said, "That is no law." Then the judge agreed with him, and he got every one of them off after that; but only for him they would swing. The Tithes were bad, a farmer to have three stacks they's take the one of them. And that was the first time of the hurling matches, to gather the people against the Tithes. But there was hurling in the ancient times in Ireland, and out in Greece, and playing at the ball, and that is what is called the Olympian Games.

RAFTERY CALLS TO THE CONNACHT MEN
TO JOIN IN THE TITHE WAR

RISE up, the fight is drawing to you; let ye have sword and spear. The lucky Five is at hand. The two provinces of Munster are afoot and will not stop till Tithes are overthrown, and rents along with them. We to stand by Ireland the English Guard would be feeble, and every gap made easy. The Gall will be on their back without ever turning, and the Orangemen bruised in the borders of every town; a judge and jury in the Courthouse for the Catholics; England dead and the crown upon the Gael. There is many a fine man at this time under sentence from Cork to Ennis and the town of Roscrea; fair-haired boys wandering and departing from the streets of Kilkenny to Bantry Bay. But the cards will turn and we'll have a good hand. The trump will stand on the board we play at. Let ye have courage. It is a fine story I have. Ye will gain the day in every quarter from the Sassanach. Let ye strike the board and the cards will be coming to you. Drink out of hand now a health to Raftery; it is he would put success for you on the cause we plead.

THE BIG WIND

As to the Big Wind, I was on my elder sister's back going to a friend beyond and when I was coming back it was slacked away, and I was wondering at the holes in the houses. I was up to twelve year at the time of the Big Wind that was in '39, and I was over at Roxborough with my father that was clearing timber from the road, and your father came out along the road, and he was wild seeing the trees and rocks whipped up into the sky the way they were with the wind. But what was that to the bitter time of the Famine that came after?

THE FAMINE

THE Famine; there's a long telling in that, it is a thing will be remembered always. That little graveyard above, at that time it was filled full up of bodies; the Union had no way to buy coffins for them. There would be a bag made, and the body put into it, that was all; and the people dying without priest, or bishop, or anything at all. But over in Connemara it was the dogs brought the bodies out of the houses, and asked no leave.

MORE ABOUT THE FAMINE

THE world is better now than what it was, for I remember the time I saw men dying out of their standing with the hunger, I seen two brothers dying in a little corner of a field, and nothing around them only the wall. I seen women watching the hen to lay an egg that they'd bring it into the market to get kitchen for

the children, and they couldn't put one on the fire. I saw three
men transported for sheepstealing, and I saw twenty-eight legs
of mutton taken out of the garden of one of them. To salt them
they did, and to put them in a cellar in the ground. It was to New
South Wales these two were sent, and they were put to work in
a gold mine. And at their death there was sent back to their family
four thousand pounds in money. But when it was got in no good
way it did not last, it went to the bad like the froth of the stream.
There was a woman in the time of the Famine and she was dying
for the want of food, and she with six or seven pounds that was
in sovereigns tied about her neck, and a farthing along with them.
But she would not break a sovereign to take a shilling out of it. And
a rat came up and ate the thread, and brought away the sovereigns
to its hole, but the farthing it left outside. That is a true story. It
is up in the mountains the woman was. There was a fool at Burren,
Egan his name was, he always went barefoot. And if I would be
praising a pair of boots he would say, "This is a better sole,"
and he would turn up the sole of his foot and say, "It lasted since
the year of the Black Potatoes," for that was the year of his birth.

AT THE TIME OF THE FAMINE

As to the Martins of Ballinahinch, there got to be a debt on it,
and Tom Martin borrowed two barrels of gold from the Law Life
Company. They were brought to the house at Ballinahinch, and
it was at the time of the Famine and Tom Martin's tenants were
carried away by the hundred to the Poorhouse at Clifden. And he
went to see did they get any sort of good attendance or nourishment, and they did not get it. And he took the fever and went
home and took to his bed and they got nurses for him. And after
his death there was no sign of the two barrels of gold. Some said
the Missis took the one of them, and it might have been the
daughter and the man she married took the other. It is the way
the estate went. The Colonel, Tom Martin's father, went travelling
through England and France and Spain and Portugal spending
money in every place. One time he stopped so long away his wife
that he left at home went away with some rich man, I forget his
name. They went to his house that was between Oughterard and
Galway. She stopped in that house and never went out of it,
fearing that Colonel Martin might come back and that if he knew
she was in it he would take the life of the man she was with. And
when the Colonel came back and found the wife gone he went
looking for her, and he never could get a sight of her because she
was shut up in the house, and he knew if he went to it he would

not be let in. He knew well she was there, but he had no proof. And one day he met with a pedlar that was carrying little things for sale in a kishoge, and he asked the pedlar to peel off his clothes and to give them to him in exchange for his own clothes. "And I might meet you some other time again," he said. So the pedlar peeled off his clothes and the Colonel put them on, and he took the kishoge and went to Galway and to—you know this yourself better than I can tell you—the best jeweller—and he filled the kishoge with every sort of gold things till it was full up, and then he went to the rich man's house and knocked at the gate and the servant girl came and opened it. He asked leave to come in then and he showed her the kishoge, and because such things as he had are dear to women, the girl let him as far as the kitchen. "Ask your mistress to come look at the things," he said then. "Oh," said the girl, "I cannot do that for she is in her bed yet." "Bring them up then to the bed," says he, "and let her make her choice." So the girl took the kishoge and went opening door after door going through the house, and the Colonel had but slippers—Oh, he was very clever! And he slipped on the slippers and went following her from door to door and she not hearing him following after her. They came then to the door where the lady was and she gave a jerk of her elbow to the man that was in the bed with her. "If Martin is living," she said, "that is him walking." The man jumped up then, and there was a table where he had three revolvers always on it. But the Colonel ran past the girl and took the revolvers from the table before he could reach them. Then he looked at his wife and at the man, and he said, "I have seen you now and I have a witness. I might shoot you now," he said, "but I never like to shoot a man in his bed." And he might have shot him, for there was no law in the country to prevent him doing it. And he turned and walked out of the house, and the gold things he had he gave them to the girl. He went then to Galway and took the law against the rich man and he took the barrel of gold from him, full of sovereigns and half sovereigns that it was past counting and went by weight. And he sent for Tim Hart that was in his employment and he said, "Get a car and drive through all the streets of Galway and scatter that to every poor person that is in the streets." So Tim Hart got the car and put the barrel on it and went scattering the gold through the streets. The rich man, now, had set a man having a pistol at every street corner to kill Colonel Martin before he could leave the town. But when they saw the great relief that came to Galway and to every poor person with the scattering of the gold their heart changed in them, and every one of them put up his pistol and turned away. Tim Hart came back and told the

Colonel he had scattered all the gold. "Did you keep none of it for yourself?" said the Colonel. "I did not," said he. "Then you will never live to be rich," said he, "where you didn't put some of it in your own pocket." And I remember my father telling me he saw Tim Hart, an old man and a poor man, gathering seaweed at that strand beyond like any other one. As to the wife, she outlived the Colonel. And when her death was near she came to her son Tom, at the house of Ballinahinch, and offered him to redeem the property if he would let her in to die at home. But he would not let her in. The Colonel was followed from Galway another time by bailiffs, and they had three of the best horses in Galway following him, but they could not come up with him on his little grey mare.

THE CHOLERA

The cholera was worse again. It came from foreign, and it lasted a couple of years, till God drove it out of the country. It is often I saw a man ploughing the garden in the morning till dinner time, and before evening he would be dead. It was as if on the wind it came, there was no escape from it; on the wind, the same as it would come now and would catch on to pigs. Sheds that would be made out in the haggards to put the sick in; they would turn as black as your coat. There was no one could go near them without he would have a glass of whiskey taken, and he wouldn't like it then.

A LONG REMEMBERING

The longest thing I remember is the time of the sickness, and my father that was making four straw mats for four brothers that died, and that couldn't afford coffins. The bodies were put in the mats and were tied up in them. And the second thing I remember is the people digging in the stubble after the oats and the wheat to see would they meet a potato, and sometimes they did, for God sent them there.

RAFTERY'S SONG FOR THE WHITEBOYS

I promise ye, whichever of ye will be living, that the "Ribbonmen" will get the price of their health they lost, sitting up every whole night under frost, under snow and under rain. There will be no rent to pay from this out of the King. There will be no talk of Tithes or anything of the sort, there will be no price on the land. The Sannanach vexed and defeated, and the Children of the

Gael will get the upper hand. Let ye stand close, let ye not go back. Let ye break your way through the Guard. There will come relief and victory to us without delay; and the Son of God will put down our enemy.

THE TERRY ALTS

THE Terry Alts were a bad class; everything you had they'd take from you. It was against herding they began to get the land, the same as at the present time. And women they would take; a man maybe that hadn't a perch of land would go to a rich farmer's house and bring away his daughter. And I, supposing, to have some spite against you, I'd gather a mob and do every bad thing to destroy you. That is the way they were, a bad class and doing bad deeds. One of them went to confession to the priest, that asked him how many crimes did he do, and he said, "I was at thirteen killings between Clare and Connacht." He met with a dreadful death. His tongue came four inches out, that neither priest nor doctor could put it in.

THE '48 TIME

THOMAS Davis was a great man where poetry is concerned, and a better than Thomas Moore. All over Ireland his poetry is, and he would have done other things but that he died young. That was the '48 time. The '48 men were foolish men; they thought to cope with the English Government. They went to O'Connell to get from him all the money he had gathered, for they had it in their head to use that to make a rise against England. But when they asked O'Connell for it he told them there was none of it left not one penny. Buying estates for his children he used it, and he said he spent it on a monastery. I don't know was he speaking truth. Mahon made a great speech against him, and it preyed on O'Connell, and he left the country and went away and died in some place called Genoa. He was a very ambitious man, like Napoleon. He got Emancipation; but where is the use of that? There's Judge O'Brien, Peter the Packer, was calling out and trying to do away with trial by jury. And he would not be in his office or in his billet if it wasn't for O'Connell. They didn't do much after, where they didn't get the money from O'Connell. And the night they joined under Smith O'Brien they hadn't got their supper. A terrible cold night it was, no one could stand against it. Some bishop came from Dublin, and he told them to go home, for

how could they reach with their pikes to the English soldiers that
had got muskets. The soldiers came, and there was some firing,
and they were all scattered. As to Smith O'Brien, there was ten
thousand pounds on his head, and he hid for a while. Then at the
last he went into the town of Clonmel, and there was a woman
there in the street was a huckster, and he bade her give him up to
the Government, for she would never earn money so easy. But for
all he was worth she wouldn't do that. So then he went and gave
himself up, and he was sent to Australia, and the property was given
to his brother. There were great inventions made in these days,
but the poems are not so good as in the old times, when Thomas
Davis was writing or Tommy Moore.

A THING MITCHELL SAID

MITCHELL was kept in Clonmel gaol two years before he was sent
to Australia. He was a Protestant, and a very good man. He said
in a speech, where was the use of meetings and of talking? It was
with the point of their bayonet the English would have to be
driven out of Ireland. It was Mitchell said that.

THE FENIAN RISING

IT was a man from America it came with. There was one Mackie
was taken in a public-house in Cork, and there was a policeman
killed in the struggle. Judge O'Hagan was the judge when he was
in the dock, and he said, "Mr. Mackie, I see you are a gentleman
and an educated man; and I'm sorry," he said, "that you did not
read Irish history." Mackie cried when he heard that, for indeed
it was all spies about him, and it was they gave him up.

A GREAT WONDER

THE greatest wonder I ever saw was one time near Kinvara at a
funeral, there came a car along the road and a lady on it having a
plaid cloak, as was the fashion then, and a big hat, and she kept
her head down and never looked at the funeral at all. I wondered
at her when I saw that, and I said to my brother it was a strange
thing a lady to be coming past a funeral and not to look on at it
at all. And who was on the car but O'Gorman Mahon, escaping
from the Government, and dressed up as a lady! He drove to
Father Arthur's house in Kinvara, and there was a boat waiting,
and a cousin of my own in it, to bring him out to a ship, and so he
made his escape.

ANOTHER WONDER

I saw Clerkenwell prison in London broken up in the time of the Fenians, and every ship and steamer in the whole of the ocean stopped. The prison was burned down, and all the prisoners consumed, and seven doctors' shops along with it.

FATHER MATHEW

Father Mathew was a great man, plump and red in the face. There couldn't be better than what he was. I knew one Kane in Gort he gave a medal to, and he kept it seventy years. Kane was a great totaller, and he wouldn't drink so much as water out of a glass, but out of a cup; the glass might have been used for porter at some time. He lost the medal and was in a great way about it, but he found it five years after in a dung-heap. A great totaller he was. Them that took the medal from Father Mathew and that kept it, at their death they would be buried by men dressed in white clothes.

THE WAR OF THE CRIMEA

My husband was in the war of the Crimea. It is terrible the hardships he went through, to be two months without going into a house, under the snow in trenches. And no food to get, maybe a biscuit in the day. And there was enough food there, he said, to feed all Ireland; but bad management, they could not get it. Coffee they would be given, and they would be cutting a green bramble to strive to make a fire to boil it. The dead would be buried every morning; a big hole would be dug, and the bodies thrown in, and lime upon them; and some of the bodies would be living when they were buried. My husband used to try to revive them if he saw there was life in them, but other lads wouldn't care—just to put them down and have done. And they were allowed to take nothing—money, gold watches, and the like, all thrown in the ground. Sure they did not care much about such things, they might be lying in the same place themselves tomorrow. But the soldiers would take the money sometimes and put it in their stocking and tie the stocking below the ankle and below the knee. But if the officer knew that, they would be court-martialed and punished. He got two medals—one from the English and one from the Emperor of Turkey. Fighting for the Queen, and bad pay she gave him. He never knew what was the war for, unless it might be for diminishing the population. We saw in the

paper a few years ago there was a great deal of money collected for
soldiers that had gone through hardship in the war, and we wrote
to the War Office asking some of it for him. But they wrote back
that there were so many young men crippled in the Boer war there
was nothing to be spared for the old. My husband used to be
saying the Queen cared nothing for the army, but that the King,
even before he was King, was better to it. But I'm thinking from
this out the King will get very few from Ireland for his army.
Stephen Burke was in the war against the Russians, three nations
against them, and they were the best of all. He'd frighten you
talking of it. Where he was they had dykes dug, and to be waiting
till the day came and as many as sheep in a field you'd see the
Russians firing.

GARIBALDI

THERE was one of my brothers died at Lyons in France. He had
a place in Guinness's brewery, and earning £3 10s. a week, and
it was the time Garibaldi, you might have heard of, was out
fighting. There came a ship to Dublin from France, calling for
soldiers, and he threw up his place, and there were many others
threw up their place, and they went off, eleven hundred of them,
in the French ship, to go fighting for their religion, and a hundred
of them never came back. When they landed in France they were
made much of and velvet carpets spread before them. But the war
was near over then, and when it had ended they were forgotten,
and nothing done for them, and he was in poverty at Lyons and
died. It was the nuns there wrote a letter in French telling that to
my mother. And Napoleon the Third fought for the Pope in the
time of Garibaldi. A great many Irishmen went out at that time,
and the half of them never came back. I met with one of them that
was in Russell's flour stores, and he said he would never go out
again if there were two hundred Popes. Bad treatment they got—
black bread, and the troops in the Vatican well fed; and it wasn't
long till Victor Emmanuel's troops made a breach in the wall.

THE BUONAPARTES

NAPOLEON the First was a great man; it was given out of him
there never would be so great a man again. But he hadn't much
education, and his penmanship was bad. Every great man gave
in to superstition. He gave into it when he went to ask the gipsy
woman to divine, and she told him his fate. Through fire and a
rock she said that he would fall. I suppose the rock was St. Helena,

and the fire was the fire of Waterloo. Napoleon was the terror of England, and he would have beat the English at Waterloo but for treachery, the treachery of Grouchy. It was, maybe, not his fault he was treacherous, he might be the same as Judas, that had his treachery settled for him four thousand years before his birth. But Boney's play was fair play. He tried to make his escape from St. Helena in a barrel. He passed two sentries but he was stopped by the third; he that had found the world too small for him. Napoleon the Third was not much. He died in England, and was buried in a country churchyard much the same as Kiltartan. There was a curse on him because of what Napoleon the First had done against the Church. He took Malta one time and landed there, and by treachery with the knights he robbed a church that was on the shore, and carried away the golden gates. In an ironclad he put them that was belonging to the English, and they sank that very day, and were never got up after, unless it might be by divers. And two Popes he brought into exile. But he was the friend of Ireland, and when he was dying he said that. His heart was smashed, he said, with all the ruling Princes that went against him; and if he had made an attack on Ireland, he said, instead of going to Moscow the time he did, he would have brought England low. And the Prince Imperial was trapped. It was the English brought him out to the war, and that made the nations go against him, and it was an English officer led him into the trap the way he never would come to the Throne.

THE ZULUS

I was in the army the time of the Zulu war. Great hardship we got in it and plenty of starvation. It was the Dutch called in the English to help them against the Zulus, that were tricky rogues, and would do no work but to be driving the cattle off the fields. A pound of raw flour we would be given out at seven o'clock in the morning, and some would try to make a cake, and some would put it in a pot with water and be stirring it, and it might be eleven o'clock before you would get what you could eat, and not a bit of meat maybe for two days.

THE YOUNG NAPOLEON

THERE was a young Napoleon there, the grandson of Napoleon the First, that was a great man indeed. I was in the island where he was interred; it is a grand place, and what is not natural in those parts, there are two blackthorn bushes growing in it where you go into the place he was buried. And as to that great Napoleon, the fear of him itself was enough to kill people. If he was living till now it is hard to say what way would the world be. It is likely there'd be no English left in it, and it would be all France. The young Napoleon was at the Zulu war was as fine a young man as you'd wish to lay an eye on; six feet four, and shaped to match. As to his death, there was things might have been brought to light, but the enquiry was stopped. There was seven of them went out together, and he was found after, lying dead in the ground, and his top coat spread over him. There came a shower of hail-stones that were as large as the top of your finger, and as square as diamonds, and that would enter into your skull. They made out it was to save himself from them that he lay down. But why didn't they lift him in the saddle and bring him along with them? And the bullet was taken out of his head was the same every bit as our bullets; and where would a Zulu get a bullet like that? Very queer it was, and a great deal of talk about it, and in my opinion he was done away with because the English saw the grandfather in him, and thought he would do away with themselves in the time to come. Sure if he spoke to one of them, he would begin to shake before him, officers the same as men. We had often to be laughing seeing that.

A DECENT WAR

THIS is not a natural war (1915), but shooting from the air and from the depths of the sea. The Zulu war was a decent war that I was in. Six hundred of the blacks we killed one time, and took eight hundred of their cattle. They were let get them back after, if they would pay seven pounds for each head of cattle, and that was divided among the soldiers. After the fight was over Lord Roberts gave us a week to enjoy ourselves, and there was a house and all ready for us. Wasn't he a great man to do that?

PARNELL

PARNELL was a very good man, and a just man, and if he had lived to now, Ireland would be different to what it is. The only thing ever could be said against him was the influence he had with that woman. And how do we know but that was a thing appointed for him by God? Parnell had a back to him, but O'Connell stood alone. He fought a good war in the House of Commons. Parnell did a great deal, getting the land. He wouldn't like at all that you'd wrong the poor. I often heard he didn't die at all—it was very quick for him to go. I often wondered there were no people smart enough to dig up the coffin and to see what is in it, at night they could do that. No one knows in what soil Robert Emmet was buried, but he was made an end of sure enough. Parnell went through Gort one day, and he called it the fag-end of Ireland, just as Lady Morgan called the North the Athens of Ireland.

THE ILL LUCK OF IRELAND

PARNELL was good, but he lost his character and disgraced his name. It was may be the ill luck of Ireland brought him in the way of that woman; set down for him it was. I heard a priest say at the altar he would go from sea to Shannon with Parnell, and that he was a man never told a lie. The priests used to go about linked with him at that time. And after the Kitty O'Shea business I knew a priest said at the altar he would not give his boots to be blacked by a Parnellite woman. What call had they to come down on him with that, and he not of their religion? They annoyed Parnell greatly. But if they did, he did wrong himself. Why couldn't he have married some lady or even a servant girl in the house? There was a friend of mine telling me he saw Captain O'Shea one time, and that he was a very fine man, a finer man than Parnell.

HIS LAST FIGHT

THE time I heard Parnell was after the priests all went against him, and he said he himself would fight it single-handed out. I heard him at a meeting in Ennis, it is one of the last he held. He was not eloquent and he was feeble at the time, but he got great cheering. I heard John Dillon speaking against him in Gort, that was at the time of the split. He brought down O'Shea's wife on him and said he ought not to be left at large. The people did not like that and they hooted at the end, and he was vexed and he said he could buy the whole of them for half a pint of porter. He gave his life and his health for the people and he had no trickery, and his grandfather like him would not be bought at the time of the Union. Gladstone threw a stone at him too. He died a bankrupt and Avondale was sold. But as to his burial, there are some say he never was buried at all. Every great man has his limit and there he must fall—that is what the High Priest came out and told Constantine that had put down all the world and that went to Jerusalem. The High Priest told him that, and when and where he would fall. And he put on him the name of the Skipping Goat.

MR. GLADSTONE

GLADSTONE had the name of being the greatest statesman of England, and he wasn't much after all. At the time of his death he had it on his mind that it was he threw the first stone at Parnell, and he confessed that, and was very sorry for it. But sure there is no one can stand all through. Look at Solomon that had ten hundred wives, and some of them the finest of women, and that spent all the money laid up by Father David. And Gladstone encouraged Garibaldi the time he attacked the Vatican, and gave him arms, Parnell charged him with that one time in the House of Commons, and said he had the documents, and he hadn't a word to say. But he was sorry at Parnell's death, and what was the use of that when they had his heart broke? Parnell did a great deal for the Irish, and they didn't care after; they are the most displeasing people God ever made, unless it might be the ancient Jews.

QUEEN VICTORIA'S RELIGION

QUEEN Victoria was loyal and true to the Pope; that is what I was told, and so is Edward the Seventh loyal and true, but he has got something contrary in his body. It is when she was a girl she put on clothes like your own—lady's clothes—and she went to the Pope. Did she turn Catholic? She'd be beheaded if she did; the Government would behead her; it is the Government has power in England.

HER WISDOM

As to the last Queen, we thought her bad when we had her, but now we think her good. She was a hard woman, and she did nothing for Ireland in the bad years; but I'll give you the reason she had for that. She had it in her mind always to keep Ireland low, it being the place she mostly got her soldiers. That might not be good for Ireland, but it was good for her own benefit. The time the lads have not a bit to eat, that is the time they will go soldiering.

WAR AND MISERY

THE old Queen never stretched out her hand to the poor, or if she did I never heard of it, and I am old enough to hear many histories. There was war and misery going on all through her reign. It was the Boer war killed her, she being aged, and seeing all her men going out, and able to do nothing. Ten to one they were against the Boers. That is what killed her. It is a great tribute to the war it did that.

KING EDWARD VII

THE present King is very good. He is a gentleman very fond of visiting, and well pleased with every class of people he will meet.

THE OLD AGE PENSIONS

THE old age pension is very good, and as to taxes, them can't pay it that hasn't it. It is since the Boer War there is coin sent back from Africa every week that is dug from the goldpits out there. That is what the English wanted the time they went to war; they want to close up the minerals for themselves. If it wasn't for the war, that pension would never be given to Ireland. They'd have been driven home by the Boers if it wasn't for the Irish that were in the front of every battle. And the Irish held out better too, they can starve better than the rest, there is more bearing in them. It wasn't till all the Irish were killed that the English took to bribing. Bribed Botha they did with a bag of gold. For all the generals in England that are any good are Irish. Buller was the last they had, and he died. They can find no good generals at all in England, unless they might get them very young.

ANOTHER THOUGHT

IT was old money was in the Treasury idle, and the King and Queen getting old wanted to distribute it in the country it was taken from. But some say it was money belonging to captains and big men that died in the war and left no will after them. Anyway it is likely it will not hold; and it is known that a great many of those that get it die very soon.

A PROPHECY

IT is likely there will be a war at the end of the two thousand, that was always foretold. And I hear the English are making ships that will dive the same as diving ducks under the water. But as to the Irish Americans, they would sweep the entire world; and England is afraid of America, it being a neighbour.

THE GREAT WAR: THE OLD PEOPLE SAY:

THERE will not be a man left in Gort. They are being tracked for the reserve and as out-soldiers. It is in Mayo the war began. There were guns in a house, and information was given and they were brought away, and those they were brought from began burning and scalding. That is the way the fight began, and now there are five nations in it. This war was prophesied hundreds of years ago by Columcille and it will not leave a man living in Ireland. The King—no one knows is he for or against it, but he is but one man and what can he do? A King has no leave to get his own way. Look at Charles the Second how they whipped the head of him. Look at the reverses Napoleon had and he got the better of them, he having a heart of marble.

UP IN SLIEVE ECHTGE

PRIESTS we have, giving a Mission, we are going there every night. They have great talk of the war. It is the English they say will be defeated and put down. They bade the boys to keep silent for a while, where a whole fleet of them, seventy or eighty, were out drilling in the fields every night. Guns they were expecting and they had clothes down. But there is no drilling since the war, and they are not in it, for they are in dread they will be brought away by the Press. And the Priest said to keep silent that they would not be brought away, and to see what way would it turn out. He talked of the Boer war too, and he said that at the end of it there used to be but two men fighting one another in a field. And it will be the same in this war he said, for they are cutting down men the same as a field of corn. I heard the old people saying Buonaparte was coming to land in Ireland one time, and when he was half way he turned back. And I pray to the Lord it will be the same with these, for they are very wicked and are killing all before them.

AN OLD MAN SAYS:

THEY say the Germans will be coming here. If they do break in I suppose we must go on their side or it'll be worse for us. But his old wife says from her bed, Ah, what about them? We have but the one death. We have not two deaths to die.

THE GERMANS

SURE the Germans marched through Paris victorious in Bismarck's time, and they demanded all before them, and the best of the ladies of Paris had to throw them out their gold bracelets. For the Germans are a terribly numerous race. MacMahon said of them they were coming up every day like a swarm of flies. Whatever number of them were killed they would be coming next day as if out of the ground, the same as a second resurrection.

THE ENGLISH LAW

A man at Duras was telling me that the English will not be put down till the time the sea will get dry, and it is as well, for without their law in the country the Irish would have one another ate and killed. But the Germans are like starlings going through the air, and the prophecy of Columcille is coming true that the time would come when an old man would be turned three times in the bed to know could he show garrison duties in the barracks and to know could he go to the war when the best soldiers would be gone. In the Crimea it was in a song that the Russians were coming on ahead, and in no dread, but that the English would put them to fear in no time.

THE GERMAN PRISONERS

I REMEMBER the war of the Crimea; it was the French gained that for the English. It was a great war and lasted two and a half years, but if it did there was only a field day once a week, but now they are fighting day and night. If I was the English I wouldn't be bringing German prisoners into England, or as they're doing in Tipperary. I'd put a bullet through the head of every damn one of them. Sure to be reading of them in the papers and the way they are killing nuns and priests would rise the hair on your head. And what nature now have they for us over the Belgians?

THE KAISER'S SON

ISN'T the Kaiser terrible to send his son out fighting till he got his death? A fine young man. It would be better have sent him on a pleasure trip to London.

THE PURPOSE OF GOD

A MAN of the name of Hanrahan was telling me the Germans have near enough of it, and it's time for them to be put down, destroying all in streets and in the deep sea. Things they have the size of turnips, and they burst up and blow all through the elements. But all that is drowned or killed or is a corpse laid down in the ground will come before God at the last day in his own uniform. Every man will be a scholar that time, and will be able to read all we did in our life, that will be written in our forehead. But it is not in the purpose of God that anyone he made would be destroyed, as it is well He earned them. And it's often I said after going to the chapel, "If it wasn't for the priests beckoning hell to us what way would they get their living? There's no one would give them a halfpenny."

IN THE PROPHECIES

ISN'T the war terrible! The oldest people in the world are saying
it is the worst that was ever in the world. It was in the prophecies
long ago. And there was a priest prophesied it would come as far
as Kilchriest and the Cross would be lifted up there and it would
stop. They are fighting out in some place where Saint John used
to be, and there is a monument to him. And the Germans were
firing night and day at that monument but they could not hit it,
and no shot anchored in it at all. I wonder will the Lord put out
His hand to stop it? And it would be a pity for it to come to Ireland,
for we had fighting enough here, and what will we do if it comes
into Ireland? And the army itself wouldn't be the worst, but the
scamps and schemers they send on ahead of them.

IN BUONAPARTE'S TIME

THIS is a terrible war—a great war. A great shame any crowned
head to have leave to bring such trouble into the world. There are
a good many going away because they are fearing to be taken in
spite of themselves. At the time of Buonaparte's wars there was
good bounties given to the recruits at one time, £21 and a bottle of
whiskey and a leg of mutton and a silver watch, all given into his
hand before ever they'd take the oath. But one day a sergeant that
was recruiting said, "If you won't take it to-day you won't get it
to-morrow." And sure enough the next day they were taken by the
Press, and put in tenders one on top of the other.

THE WAR OF BUONAPARTE

I OFTEN heard Maurteen's mother telling of the war of Buonaparte; and she said if you were hid down in the deepest hole of
Ireland you should put your head up to see that war that was the
greatest the world ever knew. £22 they would give a recruit that
time in Loughrea, and he had to go through his right hand turn
and his left hand turn. Old men the recruiting sergeant would
take, and them that were upon one arm and one leg.

THE KAISER

THE Kaiser was preparing for it this long time. He must be a
terrible man, his five sons out with the army and himself out with
it. And look at all they did in Belgium. That was the way in
ancient Rome with an Emperor they called Domitian. Killing
men all the day he was, and his valet catching flies for him to
kill at night.

THAT SON OF SAGGARTON'S

IT is a very threatening thing to go to the front of the war. In the old times they were not liable but to an odd day's war or a battle, but now they are fighting every day. It grieves me beyond measure to see that son of Saggarton's that came back dragging the foot after him. Sure they have the whole world killed, and how could you cross to America with mines and disturbances in the sea?

THE JAPS

THE Germans seemed to be making great headway, but the Austrians are making great complaints now with the scarcity of food, the bread so stale that they cannot stand with it. It is looking better now. The Japs are after giving them a sweep and it is likely all the other nations will give them a sweep. And indeed it is time to give them a check with their spies all over the world in every port and place.

KITCHENER'S MEN

THE Germans are showing some slacking, but they're strong enough yet. Sure they were educated to the army, not like Kitchener's million men that if you would put a gun in their hand wouldn't hit a haycock. A lad that went out and came back was telling me if you put an egg on your head and let it fall it would frighten them. Devilment in the air and devilment on the earth and under the sea. It is the greatest war I ever saw. It has played with the world entirely; the people are all out of time. There is no one rightly ruined by it only the wretched poor.

THE CAUSE OF THE WAR

IT is a good job the Germans are beat. Sure the Almighty God wouldn't be above without he'd have revenge on them. As to what brought about the war, there was too much of a population in it, and they wanted to gain more ground and they drew the war. Diving boats they have and flyboats in the air. The Kaiser thought he'd walk the world, like Napoleon at Waterloo. He drew a lot of trouble, he drew all that. There wouldn't be a just God in heaven if he didn't go mad or cut his throat.

ANOTHER OPINION

IT was King George they say that got up the war. The Kaiser said that himself, that it was all settled at the daughter's wedding.

WANDERING MARY SAYS:

THE war is terrible; there is a whole lot of nations carry on there that they didn't know at all. Indians there are in it, and the men from that island near America that is called Canada. But the English are very headstrong and they'll put them down yet. There is a priest going out there, a great man out and out. He says he'll go through them and he'll lose his life but he'll change them. He'll take the flag before them and the colours. That priest will hold up the Cross before them and they'll die like chickens. They cannot break in on Ireland, there's a great victory turning against them. The Gipsies (Germans) is terrible; they are worse than the blacks, going up in the air and firing down and knocking. Worse than the blacks they are, it's of the Gipsies they got no good at all. I'm afraid it will do away with a great deal of people; the war is very bad and very strong. The Gipsies would not kill you out, they would only wound you. It's short God Almighty will be doing away with it, if some nation will come in and cut them down. There never since the world came a world was such a great war as this war. They are fighting night and day; all the men in Ireland will be brought out. They'll be pressed in the houses. Where there's three two will be taken, and where there's two one will be taken. There is not a house in the world but they're going out; sure I saw them going yesterday through Gort, knotted with bows and bits of paper upon their neck, and knots that is on their tails. It is the officers and the big heads and the gentlemen the Gipsies do be knocking. Lord Gough's son is in the hospital; it was the Gipsies that came at him. Knocking officers the way they'll break in on Ireland, that's the reason the war began. It's the biggest war that ever God created, knocking them down like chickens. Guns they have and balls filled with fire, they can shoot them as far as Loughrea. We'll be destroyed if they come to Ireland. There is nothing to save us unless that Ireland is blessed. The Pope even is blessing it. Sure out in foreign there is snakes and dirty things going about in it. I hope they will not destroy us, if the Lord gets settlement at all.

AGAIN:

THE Gipsies are terrible; didn't they burn the three best towns of England; they to break with Ireland they'll burn it the same as England and put it up into the air. That building was the best out in the blessed land; three hundred years it was building and I don't know was it four or five; the best building out in France it was. They blew it and broke it down. There is many a sore heart through them; they are the terriblest swarm that ever came in the world.

AGAIN:

HOULIHAN that went to the war yesterday, it's not likely he'll come back; he was frightened going; he is a weighty man. A handy man he was, he'd slate the house for you; shearing people and cutting the hair: he'd wash the dogs for the curates or turn down their bed, and shave the dead without charge. Down the lane they're lonesome after Houlihan. Terrible they are, there's not a ship going over or hither but they'll drown; it's on the paper the witness of it, they'll be drowned and swallowed down. There's no settlement or nothing, but always, always slaughtering. To die natural, and the priest and the doctor beside the bed, and a beautiful coffin after; what is that beside being thrown and murdered and killed and dead without shriving or a coffin, or to be drowned and swallowed down. It was prophesied women would reap the harvest, but God help the harvest women'll reap! What way could I myself take a hook in my hand? Sooner than to die by drowning I would face a bullet and ten guns. If ever I heard I was to get my death in that way I would pray to the Almighty to shoot me. They are going up in the air knocking down ships. It is the war that you never heard such a war in your life!

THE BLACK AND TANS

THERE did two carloads of the Black and Tans come into the town late yesterday evening, they were a holy fright, shouting and firing. They broke into houses and searched them, and they searched the people in the street, women and girls too that were coming out from the chapel, that they came running down the street and in dread of their life. Then they went into Flanagan's to drink and got drunk there. It is terrible to let them do that. Look at Mahon's, they burned all the bedding in the house and every bit of money he had. And at Joyce's the same way, burned all in the house and nine acres of oats. They would have burned the hay but didn't see it. Mr. Martyn's beautiful hall they didn't leave a stone of, and at Ardrahan the same way as at Mahon's they kept the boys running up and down the road for near an hour and a half, and they all but naked where they were chasing them up and down, and the girls the same way. It is a holy crime. It is worse than Belgium. What call have they coming to us that have such a quiet little town?

SOME BAD WORK

THERE was some bad work last night. Those Black and Tans that were in Clarenbridge went on to Maree that is a couple of miles further. They dragged three men out of their houses there, and shot them. They are not dead, they are wounded. Then they set fire to some of the houses and burned them down. They are savages; they are out for robbery.

A BURNING

THE party that attacked the forge came about midnight. They began firing into the kitchen through the windows, but by the mercy of God no one was there. They broke in then and dragged the boys out, dragged them all out and set fire to the house. One of the soldiers told the wife to go back and save her money and her clothes and she was going in but a policeman dragged her back. They saved nothing at all. The Old Police are ashamed of them. They stopped a man the other day turning up the road and robbed him of fifty pounds. He had just sold his calves and was bringing the price of them home.

A SCOURGING

A MAN I had known this long time, an old Land Leaguer, came to the dispensary to get his back treated. I think there was hardly a worse scourging given to our Lord—the whole back black and blue with bruises and the blood drawn in some places. It was on the side of Slieve Echtge at Peterswell that happened. Other men there were beaten, one of them was thrown on a dungheap. A Black and Tan put one foot on his face to press it into the dung and another on his stomach, and then he and the others that were treated in the same way were thrown into the village well to wash themselves.

WANDERING MARY'S THOUGHTS ABOUT THE BLACK AND TANS

TERRIBLE people the Black and Tans are in Gort and on the roads. Robbing and shooting, and to break down a house and to kill the man in it. They rob the shops and kill the people; you can't have a penny piece in your pocket. What makes them bad? Sure the badness being in themselves. To blacken their faces and their hands, and having revolvers in their pockets; their faces blacked as black as the bottom of them pots. Gort that's the quietest place in Ireland, and look what they did to Mrs. Quinn. The nicest woman that ever breathed was Mrs. Quinn to the poor. They can't be in it for ever, the police have a watch on them. There never was such a woeful time in my memory. You never seen the world the way it is now at all.

THE LONESOME ROAD

THEY are terrible in Gort, and out and firing down the second next boreen near Kelly's, and out on the borders of the town; and if they got people down the lonesome road what would they care about them? I was out gathering a faggot for the fire and two of them came up to me, soldiers, having black gaiters, and guns up to their shoulders. "Have you any money?" they said. "I have not," I said; "I haven't one penny if you gave me Ireland." "I wonder you wouldn't have some ha'pence to give us," they said. But when they saw I had nothing they went away.

SHE HAS HEARD GENERAL SMUTS IS COMING

THERE will be peace. And there's a man coming in the skies, a fine gentleman to see is Ireland all right. Sure in Gort you cannot be out in the evening, and you have to close down; and maybe you'll be shot through the door. It is terrible to see innocent children falling and roaring for want of earnings. And if the men are earning itself and out late they'll be shot. And the priests themselves afraid of their lives to go out of a night. There's damnation before you on the road; they'll hide in corners like wisps and be firing out at you. They left me when I had no money. What could they do with my body? Buckles round their waists, and shoes of different colours, red shoes and white. I don't like the way they are. The time they go out on horses there's a General before them and a General behind, and he having a sword on each side of him. Down the country and up about Connemara the people cannot sleep in the houses; they would be burned over them. It is a terrible time. You'd be afraid to be out late in Gort; you'd be afraid to be coming home. The man in the skies is settling down things; he is coming from very far out; from South Africa or maybe from India. There is gold buckles all over his clothes; there is gold rings in his ears. He'll settle down everything and he'll begin work. All drink will be stopped. Ah, let me alone! He is going through the world, through the skies above, and there is no one will see him till the day he'll land in Ireland.

AN OLD MAN'S PROPHECY (1923)

I TELL you the English will be back again and this Government put out. It is certain they will come back. It is in Columcille's prophecy. There was a Lord one time was with O'Brien in Dromoland, and O'Brien promised him whatever he would ask and he said, "Give me the house of Dromoland and the lands." So he agreed to that. But then he said he had some request to make, and the Lord said he would give it. And he said, "Give me the house and the lands of Dromoland back again"; and he had to give it. That will be the way with the English. They gave up Ireland, but they have their two eyes fixed on it, till they will get it back again.

SOME BROADSHEETS BALLADS OF
THE WARS

THE BLACKBIRD

On a fair summer's morning of soft recreation,
  I heard a fair lady a-making great moan;
With sighing and sobbing and sad lamentation,
  A-saying "My Blackbird most royal is flown.
My thoughts they deceive me, reflections do grieve me,
  And I am overburdened with sad misery;
Yet if death it should blind me as true love inclines me,
  My Blackbird I'd seek out wherever he be.

"Once in fair England my Blackbird did flourish,
  He was the chief flower that in it did spring;
Prime ladies of honour his person did nourish,
  Because that he was the true son of a king.
But this false fortune, which still is uncertain,
  Has caused this parting between him and me.
His name I'll advance in Spain and in France;
  And I'll seek out my Blackbird wherever he'll be.

"The birds of the forest they all met together—
  The Turtle was chosen to dwell with the Dove;
And I am resolved in fair or foul weather,
  In winter or in spring for to seek out my love.
He is all my heart's treasure, my joy and my pleasure,
  And justly my love, my heart shall follow thee;
He is constant and kind, and courageous of mind;
  And bliss to my Blackbird wherever he be.

"In England my Blackbird and I were together,
  Where he was still noble and generous of heart;
And woe to the time that he first went from hither,
  Alas, he was forced from thence to depart;
In Scotland he is deemed, and highly esteemed,
  In England he seemed a stranger to be;
Yet his name shall remain in France and in Spain;
  All bliss to my Blackbird wherever he be.

"It is not the ocean can fright me with danger,
For though like a pilgrim I wander forlorn,
I may still meet with friendship from one that's a stranger
Much more than from one that in England was born.
Oh Heaven so spacious, to England be gracious,
Though some there be odious both to him and to me;
Yet joy and renown and laurel shall crown
My Blackbird with honour wherever he be."

At the time of Sarsfield and the Wild Geese

SHULE AROON

I wish I were on yonder hill,
It's there I'd sit and cry my fill,
Till every tear would turn a mill.
 Shule aroon, go gently, my love.

I'll sell my rock, I'll sell my reel,
I'll sell my only spinning wheel.
To buy for my love a sword of steel:
 Shule aroon, go gently, my love.

I'll dye my petticoats, I'll dye them red,
And round the world I'll beg my bread,
Until my parents shall wish me dead,
 Shule aroon, go gently, my love.

I wish, I wish, I wish in vain,
I wish I had my heart again,
And vainly think I'd not complain:
 Shule aroon, go gently, my love.

But now my love has gone to France,
To try his fortune to advance;
If e'er he comes back it's but a chance.
 Shule aroon, go gently, my love.

In Buonaparte's time

THE BALLAD UNIVERSALLY KNOWN AS
THE BANKS OF THE NILE

The drums are beating, love, no longer can I stay,
There's the bugle sounding that call I must obey;
We are ordered out to Portsmouth, many a long mile,
To join the British army on the Banks of the Nile.

Willie, dearest Willie, do not leave me here to mourn—
You will make me curse and rue the day that ever I was born;
For the parting from you, my love, is the parting of my life,
So stay at home, dear Willie, and I will be your wife.

Oh, Nancy, lovely Nancy, that's a thing that can't be so,
For our Colonel he gave orders that no woman there can go;
We must forsake our own sweethearts, likewise our native soil,
To fight the Blacks and Negroes on the Banks of the Nile.

Then I'll cut off my yellow locks and go along with you,
I'll dress myself in velvet and gold and see the Captain too;
I will fight and bear your banner while fortune on us will smile,
And we'll comfort one another on the banks of the Nile.

Your waist it is too slender and your fingers are too small.
I fear you would not answer me when on you I would call;
Your delicate constitution would not bear the unwholesome
  clime—
The hot and sandy deserts on the banks of the Nile.

My curse attend the war and the hour it began,
For it has robbed old Ireland of many a gallant man;
It took from me my own sweetheart, the protection of our soil,
And their bloodstreams the grass does steep on the banks of the
  Nile.

But when the war is over it's home we will return,
To our wives and sweethearts we left behind to mourn;
We'll embrace them in our arms until the end of time,
And we'll go no more to battle on the banks of the Nile.

THE GREEN LINNET

Curiosity led a young native of Erin to view the gay banks of the
  Rhine,
Where an Empress he saw. And the robe she was wearing all
  over with diamonds did shine;
No goddess in splendour was ever yet seen to equal this fair maid
  so mild and serene,
In soft murmurs she cried, "Oh, my Linnet so green, Sweet
  Boney, will I ne'er see you more?

"The cold frosty Alps you freely passed over, which Nature had
  placed in your way:
At Marengo, Bellona around you did hover; all Paris rejoiced the
  next day.

It grieves me the hardships you did undergo; the mountains you
  traversed all covered with snow,
And the balance of power your courage laid low: Sweet Boney,
  will I ne'er see you more?

"The crowned heads of Europe they were in great splendour and
  swore they would have you submit;
But the goddess of freedom soon made them surrender, and
  lowered their standards to your wit.
Old Frederick's colours to France you did bring; his offspring
  found shelter under your wing;
That year at Vienna you sweetly did sing: Sweet Boney, will I
  ne'er see you more?

"What numbers of men there were eager to slay you! Their
  malice you viewed with a smile;
Their gold though all Europe was found to betray you;
  they joined with the Mamelukes on the Nile.
Like ravenous vultures their vile passions did burn; the orphans
  they slew and caused widows to mourn;
But my Linnet is gone and he ne'er will return: Sweet Boney,
  will I ne'er see you more?

"I ranged through the deserts of wild Abyssinia, and could yet
  find no cure for my pain;
I will go and inquire at the isle of St. Helena, but soft whispers
  murmur ' 'Tis vain.'
Come, tell me, ye critics, come, tell me in time, what nations
  I'll rove my Green Linnet to find; was he slain at Waterloo,
  in Spain or on the Rhine?
No; he's dead on St. Helena's bleak shore."

In the ninety-eight time

THE CROPPY BOY

'Twas early, early, all in the spring,
The pretty small birds began to sing;
They sang so sweet and so gloriously,
And the tune they played was sweet liberty.

'Twas early, early, last Thursday night,
The yeoman cavalry gave me a fright;
The fright they gave was to my downfall:
I was prisoner taken by Lord Cornwall.

'Twas in his guardhouse I was confined,
And in his parlour I was closely tried;
My sentence passed and my spirits low,
And to Duncannon I was forced to go.

My sister Mary, in deep distress,
She ran downstairs in her morning dress,
Five hundred pounds she would lay down
To see me walking through Wexford town.

As I was walking the hills so high,
Who could blame me if I did cry;
With a guard behind me and another before,
And my tender mother crying more and more?

So farewell father, and mother too,
And sister Mary, I have but you;
And if e'er I chance to return home
I'll whet my pike on those yeomen's bones.

FATHER MURPHY

At Boleyvogue as the sun was setting o'er the green meadows of
   Shelmaliere,
A rebel band set the heather blazing and brought the neighbours
   from far and near.
Then Father Murphy, from old Kilcormick, spurred up the rock
   with a warning cry,
"Arm, arm," he cried, "for I've come to lead you. Now priest
   and people must fight or die!"

He led us on against the coming soldiers, the cowardly yeomen
   he put to flight;
Down at the Harrow the boys of Wexford showed Bookey's
   regiment how men could fight.
Look out for hirelings, King George of England, search every
   kingdom that breeds a slave;
For Father Murphy, of the County Wexford, sweeps o'er the
   earth like a mighty wave.

We took Camolin and Enniscorthy, and Wexford storming
   drove out our foes;
'Twas at Slieve Coiltha our pikes were reeking with the crimson
   stream of the beaten Yeos.

At Tubberneering and Ballyellis full many a Hessian lay in his
gore.
Oh, Father Murphy, had aid come over, the green flag floated
from shore to shore.

At Vinegar Hill, on the pleasant Slaney, our heroes vainly
stood back to back,
But the Yeos at Tulla took Father Murphy and burned his body
upon the rack.
God give you glory, brave Father Murphy, and open heaven to
all your men;
The cause that called you may call to-morrow, in another war
for the green again!

In the War of the Crimea

THE FAVOURITE BALLAD ENTITLED THE
ADVENTURES OF DARBY AND JERRY

Now all you warriors draw near, and you sportsmen too,
And I'll sing six or seven good verses for you;
It's all about two fine sons that enlisted from me,
And that went to fight the Russians out in the Crimea.

The reason that they listed I'll tell all about,
Was the selling of a load of turf, they went and drank it out,
But my son Darby swore he would have revenge for that,
So he went to seek his fortune upon the very spot.

Now, said Darby to Jerry, I will have you come away
And go and fight the Russians out in the Crimea;
For if you stay at home you won't have an ounce of luck,
For bread and beef is better, boy, than supping India buck.

So we blackened up our brogues and went straight away;
And we never cried crack till we got to Belfast Quay;
And there we spied two sergeants walking up the street,
And for to take the shilling we ran up the two to meet.

When we came up to them we made the bargain on the spot,
That we'd go and fight the Russians, let us be killed or not;
So they gave to us the shilling and then to us did say,
To the right-about-face, you're bound for the Crimea.

The minute that we landed sure the war was raging hot,
And we went to take Sebastopol upon the very spot.
Like devils we kept shooting at big heaps of stones,
And my brother Jerry lost his head and I lost my marrow bones.

When the war it was over and the Russians did retreat,
I got a pair of wooden legs that fitted me complete;
But when I looked around me my brother Jem I spied,
With his head hanging down and his knapsack by his side.

O, but who'll cut the turf, ay, or who'll mow the hay?
Ay, or who'll shear the corn since Jemmy went away?
O Jemmy, lovely Jemmy, weren't you a mortal fool
For to go and dash your brains out against Sebastopol.

Now it's for my sweetheart, Maggie, what will she think of me,
That I lost my two legs far off in the Crimea?
If I ask her hand in marriage, she will say, "You silly goose,
Sure a man without his legs to a woman is no use."

So cheer up, my boys, I hear we'll shortly have good fun,
For all the old women are going to take the gun;
Now they must be full accoutred with a bustle on their back,
For to go and fight the Russian bear and stand the grand attack.

The Boer War

A MOTHER'S LAMENT FOR HER SON

One evening late, when friends did meet, I heard a mother say,
"My child, my son, my chief support, alas, is gone away;
Hard I had to rear him since the day his father died,
Happy, happy would I be if he were by my side.

"He joined the Munster Fusileers, a brave and active corps,
I little thought they'd send him out to tamper with the Boer;
From the day that he enlisted he sent me half his pay—
I'd give up what the Queen is worth to see my son to-day.

"I gave him my blessing leaving Queenstown Quay,
With many more young Irish boys to cross the raging sea;
Many a mother now in Cork is in grief as well as me,
To think the son she cared and reared, his face she'll never see.

"When the battle rages fiercely our boys are in the van;
How I do wish the blows they struck were for dear Ireland;
But duty calls, they must obey and fight against the Boer,
And many a cheerful Irish lad will fall to rise no more.

"I wish my boy was home again, oh, how I'd welcome him;
With sorrow I'm heartbroken, my eyes are growing dim.
The war is dark and cruel, but whoever wins the fight,
I pray to save my noble lad and God defend the right!

"Mothers, wives and sweethearts, cheer up and do not fret,
The men who are out in Africa we hope to see them yet.
Money plenty will be sent to help each family
From those who are in the battlefield before the enemy.

"Sisters, wives and mothers should offer up a prayer
For those who are in South Africa, the friends we loved so dear;
God be their protection, shield them from the foe,
Many of them alive to-day I fear will be laid low."

THE POOR OLD MAN

God bless and save all here, says the poor old man,
If allowed to take a chair, says the poor old man,
Some few words I'd like to say on the topic of the day,
It will pass an hour away, says the poor old man.

Aren't the Boers a noble race, says the poor old man,
Such an army for to face, says the poor old man,
Such men don't fear to die, Independence is their cry,
It's enough to make me sigh, says the poor old man.

Now De Wet is all the rage, says the poor old man,
They can't get him in the cage, says the poor old man,
We're told they're on his heel, yet he slips through like an eel,
And the lead he makes them feel, says the poor old man.

Now the only child I reared, says the poor old man,
Great Britain has not spared, says the poor old man,
But if my only child in freedom's cause had died,
I could think of him with pride, says the poor old man.

What has England sent to me? says the poor old man,
A few lines of sympathy, says the poor old man,
To say it's with regret they inform me of his death,
That's the way they pay their debt, says the poor old man.

What's poor Ireland to gain, says the poor old man,
For her children who were slain, says the poor old man,
Some millions she must pay a noble foe to slay,
But there'll come a time some day, says the poor old man.

The mills of God grind slow, says the poor old man,
And the seed the tyrants sow, says the poor old man,
They will have to reap some day, with Russia in the fray,
Who an old debt longs to pay, says the poor old man.

Now I'll say farewell to all, says the poor old man,
And the next time that I'll call, says the poor old man,
I'll have something to unfold that'll make your blood run cold,
It's a pity that I'm old, says the poor old man.

The Great War: 1914

AN IRISH MOTHER'S LAMENT

On Saturday night, when friends met, a mother did say,
"My son, my child and chief support, he is gone away;
And happy would I be to-day if he were by my side.
He joined the 18th Royal Irish, a smart and active corps,
And now he is at the Front where German cannons roar.

He left his good employment—many as well as he,
And went out to the battlefield to fight England's enemy;
I wish my boy was home again, how I'd welcome him;
My heart is bursting with grief, my eyes are growing dim.
Many a mother in Erin's isle is grieved as well as me,
Thinking of the child she reared his face no more she'd see.

At every new engagement the Irish will be there,
Always foremost in the fray, always doing their share.
Amongst the dead and dying our boys are to be seen
Fighting for the weak ones and their little Isle so green.

May Heaven bring him back to me from the Hunnish band,
Safe to his dear old mother, back to his native land."
The shot and shell are roaring as hundreds deplore,
And many a cheerful Irish lad has fallen to rise no more.

Widows, wives and orphans, cheer up and do not fret,
For the boys who are at the front we will see them yet.
Plenty of money will be sent to support each family
Whilst Irishmen are fighting against England's enemy.

Mothers, wives and orphans, I hope you'll breathe a prayer
For poor sons on the battlefield and do not shed a tear.
For God is their protection and will save them from the foe,
But many a mother's hard-reared son is in a trench laid low.

1915

THE IRISH VOLUNTEERS

Arise, you gallant young Irishmen, and ring the land with cheers;
Hurrah! Hurrah! at last we've formed the Irish Volunteers;
And every man who loves his land with rifle forth he will go
For Erin's laws and Home Rule cause against the Orange foe.

O Carson thought his Ulster bluff would Irishmen dismay,
But now we have a brighter and better day;
For Munster men, Leinster men and Connaught men are here,
Already fit for action in the Irish Volunteers.

Too long we were trampled under foes, insulted and belied,
But an Irishman can soon stop that with a rifle by his side;
And if it is fighting they want, begob, from Bombay to Cape Clear,
They will find the hardest nuts to crack are the Irish Volunteers.

Success to brave John Redmond, who still pulls at the oar;
He will steer the ship to College Green and never leave it more,
And when we have our Parliament you will see the guns and
    spears
Defiant in the sunlight by Irish Volunteers.

So hearty lads of Erin join the National Brigade;
Take every drill and out the bill and never be afraid;
For you never know what other foe you will meet in future years,
But keep the foe subdued at home, brave Irish Volunteers.

Down with Carson and his brawling crowd, their day of power
    is o'er;
Although it took some hundred years, it's broken for evermore.
Bad luck go with ascendency, it died without a tear;
Emmet shed his blood for Ireland, boys, success to the Volunteers.

Hurrah again for the National Cause, the cause that cannot die,
For coffins, ships, gibbets, starvation they did try.
But we'll tell to England straight, let her lend her mind to hear
Our National spirit she can't break while there is an Irish
    Volunteer.

So Irishmen and Irish boys join the ranks and join them soon,
And, please God, you will see us marching to the Rising of the
    Moon;
We will have Home Rule for Ireland, in spite of Carson's gang
    of Peers,
And our liberty we will maintain by the Irish Volunteers.

1916: After the rising

THE MEN OF EASTER WEEK

As children of a suffering land we always look with pride
On those who for our country's cause have nobly fought and
  died;
The men who strove from age to age to set their country free,
And perished on the battlefield or on the scaffold-tree;
And now with those who thus repose we'll reckon all who bled
Our chains to break in Easter week, with Ireland's Martyred
  Dead.

For ne'er is Ireland's glorious list full writ or nigh complete,
Until it tell of fearless men who fell in Dublin's street,
And raised once more with hopeful hearts our country's flag on
  high,
And showed that Ireland still has sons prepared to do or die.
And on our future history's page an epoch bright they'll mark;
To head that band for aye will stand McDonough, Pearse and
  Clarke.

We'll tell of Heuston, Plunkett; Kent and Connolly we'll name:
Whose names as heroes e'er will shine on Ireland's roll of fame.
McDermott, Mallin, Hanrahan, Daly, Colbert and McBride
Are men who for our country's cause have nobly bled and died.
It shows to-day that come what may our country always bred,
Hearts true and bold, like those of old, our country's martyred
  dead.

Then, brothers all, be proud of those who fell in Easter week,
Be yours the task upon their foes a vengeance dire to wreak;
Resolve to-day within your hearts, some day your faith to show,
When Freedom's slogan calls again to deal a gallant blow.
For the blood of men must flow again though orphans' tears are
  shed,
Till a nation free the shrine shall be of Ireland's Martyred Dead.

1917

THE GRAND OUL' DAME BRITANNIA

Ah! Ireland, sure I'm proud of you,
Says the Grand Oul' Dame Britannia,
To poor little Belgium, tried and true,
Says the Grand Oul' Dame Britannia,

For ye don't believe the Sinn Fein lies,
And ye know that each Gael that for England dies
Will enjoy Home Rule in the clear blue skies,
Says the Grand Oul' Dame Britannia.

Sure it often made me proud blood boil,
Says the Grand Oul' Dame Britannia,
When they tried to make out you were still disloyal,
Says the Grand Oul' Dame Britannia,
But Redmond's proved to be good and great,
He's a pillar of the English State—
Who fears to speak of ninety-eight?
Says the Grand Oul' Dame Britannia.

You want a pound or two from me,
Says the Grand Oul' Dame Britannia,
For your oul' Hibernian Academy,
Says the Grand Oul' Dame Britannia,
But you know we've got the Huns to quell,
And we want the cash for shot and shell;
Your artists (?) let them go to Hell!
Says the Grand Oul' Dame Britannia.

The Castle's now an altered place,
Says the Grand Oul' Dame Britannia,
It's the drawing-room of the Irish race,
Says the Grand Oul' Dame Britannia,
John Redmond to the throne is bowed,
'Mid a frantic cheering Irish crowd—
Great! It's like the days of Shane the Proud,
Says the Grand Oul' Dame Britannia.

Oh! Johnny Redmond, you're the boy,
Says the Grand Oul' Dame Britannia,
You're England's pride and you're Ireland's joy,
Says the Grand Oul' Dame Britannia,
For he went to France and he faced the Hun,
Then he turned around and he fired a gun—
Faix, you should have seen the Germans run,
Says the Grand Oul' Dame Britannia.

And Redmond, now Home Rule has won,
Says the Grand Oul' Dame Britannia,
And he's finished what Wolfe Tone begun,
Says the Grand Oul' Dame Britannia,

Yet rebels through the country stalk,
Shouting "Sixty-seven" and "Bachelors' Walk"—
Did you ever hear such foolish talk,
Says the Grand Oul' Dame Britannia.

Oh! Scholars, Hurlers, Saints and Bards,
Says the Grand Oul' Dame Britannia,
Come along and 'list in the Irish Guards,
Says the Grand Oul' Dame Britannia,
Each man that treads on a German's feet
Will be given a parcel tied up neat—
Of a tombstone cross and a winding sheet!
Says the Grand Oul' Dame Britannia.

September 1917

"A PRAYER WRITTEN IN MOUNTJOY PRISON, BY THOMAS ASHE, WHO DIED FOR IRELAND"

Let me carry Your Cross for Ireland, Lord,
    The hour of her trial draws near,
And the pangs and the pain of the sacrifice
    May be borne by comrades dear.
But, Lord, take me from the offering throng,
    There are many far less prepared,
Though anxious and all as they are to die
    That Ireland may be spared.

Let me carry Your Cross for Ireland, Lord,
    My cares in this world are few,
And few are the tears will fall for me
    When I go on my way to You.
Spare, oh spare, to their loved ones dear
    The brother and son and sire,
For the cause that we love may never die
    In the land of our heart's desire!

Let me carry Your Cross for Ireland, Lord,
    Let me suffer the pain and shame,
I bow my head to their rage and hate,
    And I take on myself the blame.
Let them do with my body whate'er they will.
    My spirit I offer to You,
That the faithful few who heard her call
    May be spared to Roisin Dhu.

Let me carry Your Cross for Ireland, Lord,
  For Ireland weak with tears,
For the aged man of the clouded brow,
  And the child of tender years;
For the empty homes of her golden plains,
For the hopes of her future too!
Let me carry Your Cross for Ireland, Lord!
  For the cause of Roisin Dhu.

1918

KEVIN BARRY

In Mountjoy on Monday morning,
  High upon the gallows tree,
Kevin Barry gave his young life
  For the cause of Liberty.
But a lad of eighteen summers,
  Yet no one can deny,
As he walked to death that morning
  He proudly held his head on high.

Another martyr for old Ireland,
  Another murder for the Crown,
Whose brutal laws may kill the Irish,
  But can't keep their spirits down.
Lads like Barry are no cowards,
  From the foe they will not fly,
Lads like Barry will free Ireland,
  For her sake they'll live and die.

Just before he faced the hangman,
  In his dreary prison cell,
British soldiers tortured Barry
  Just because he would not tell
The names of his brave companions
  And other things they wished to know—
"Turn informer or we'll kill you"—
  Kevin Barry answered, "No."

Calmly standing to "attention,"
  While he bade his last farewell
To his broken-hearted mother,
  Whose grief no one can tell.
For the cause he proudly cherished
  This sad parting had to be,
Then to death walked softly smiling,
  That old Ireland might be free.

March 1919

A MOUNTJOY DITTY

I'll sing you a ditty of Dublin's fair city,
   And a place called Mountjoy which all of you know.
'Twas here, of all places, the boys cut the traces,
   And got out of prison alive, alive O!

The first was bold Barton, when he was departin',
   Left a note for the Boss his politeness to show,
And a dummy in order to fool the poor warder,
   But Barton had hopped it alive, alive O!

J. J. Walsh and Pierce Beasley the trick did quite easily,
   Some pro-German devils a ladder did throw;
Then some twenty Sinn Feiners like acrobat trainers,
   Scaled the wall and got free all alive, alive O!

They're thinking to-morrow to call it Mount Sorrow,
   It's made of John Bull such a terrible show;
His prisons no longer have bolts any stronger
   To hold in Sinn Feiners alive, alive O!

I'll finish my rhyme now and think it's near time now,
   The people are all laughing wherever they go;
It caused great elation in this ancient nation—
   Sinn Feiners, pro-Irish, alive, alive O!

1920

THE BOULD BLACK AND TAN

Says Lloyd-George to Macpherson, "I give you the sack,
To uphold law and order you haven't the knack,
I'll send over Greenwood, a much stronger man,
An' fill up the Green Isle with the bould Black and Tan."

He sent them all over to pillage and loot
And burn down the houses, the inmates to shoot.
"To re-conquer Ireland," says he, "is my plan
With Macready and Co. and his bould Black and Tan."

The town of Balbriggan they've burned to the ground
While bullets like hailstones were whizzing around;
And women left homeless by this evil clan.
They've waged war on children, the bould Black and Tan.

K.B.—10

From Dublin to Cork and from Thurles to Mayo
Lies a trail of destruction wherever they go;
With England to help and fierce passions to fan,
She must feel very proud of her bould Black and Tan.

Ah, then not by the terrors of England's foul horde,
For ne'er could a nation be ruled by the sword;
For our country we'll have yet in spite of her plan,
Or ten times the number of bould Black and Tan.

We defeated Conscription in spite of their threats,
And we're going to defeat ould Lloyd-George and his pets;
For Ireland and freedom we're here to a man,
And we'll humble the pride of the bould Black and Tan.

December 1921

A "FREE STATE" JINNY-JO!

I went to see David, to London to David,
  I went to see David and what did he do?
He gave me a Free State, a nice little Free State,
  A Free State that's tied up with Red, White and Blue.

I brought it to Dublin to show to Dail Eireann,
  I brought it to Dublin and what did they do?
They asked me what kind of a thing was a Free State,
A Free State that's tied up with Red, White and Blue.

Three-quarters of Ireland a nation—I told them,
  Tied on to the Empire with Red, White and Blue;
And an oath they must swear to King George and Queen Mary,
  An oath they must swear to the son-in-law new.

I'm teaching them Irish and painting their boxes
  All over with green, sure what more can I do?
Yet they tell me they want just an Irish Republic
  Without any trimmings of Red, White and Blue!

NOTES

I HAVE given this book its name because it is in this Barony of Kiltartan that I have heard the greater number of the stories, from beggars, pipers, travelling men, at my own door; or by the road-side or in the Workhouse, though others I have been given to the north of Galway Bay, in Connemara, or on its southern shore.

I WROTE in the preface to my book of *Visions and Beliefs* that is concerned with the invisible kingdom of the Sidhe, "the Others," the faery people: "To gather folklore one needs I think patience, reverence, and a good memory." It was to help Mr. Yeats in his work at that time I began to gather the stories, but as time went on I found many pages of my copybooks were filled with legends of the Fianna and of the Saints; and then of the history of the country from the time of the English invasion and conquest, more definite, yet taking colour and shape in the minds of the people or in the poets' passionate songs. Some of the stories of the Fianna I used in *Gods and Fighting Men,* and some from Christian times in *Saints and Wonders,* and the yet later ones in the first edition of this *Kiltartan History Book,* the plates and remaining copies of which were burned during the Rising of 1916.

I HAVE now added to it many little chapters, written down in these later years, and also I have made for it a few translations from the poems of Raftery or of the Munster poets made in troubled times.

THE little book was liked; I have always claimed the right to praise it because there is not in it one word of my own: all comes from the lips of the people. Sir John Rhys spoke of it as a model for all future histories; and has not much of Plutarch come from the same source?

ALMOST all the old people who gave me the stories have now passed away. The old man who prophesied the return of the English was angry that day because he had heard a rumour his old age pension was to be reduced, but I am happy to know it was left untouched. He often found his way to my door until last summer after a few days' illness he died. And it was also in this last year that Wandering Mary's restless journeys ceased.

I MIGHT perhaps have better named the little book Myths in the Making.

A SOCIABLE people given to conversation and belief; no books in the house, no history taught in the schools; it is likely that must have been the way of it in old Greece, when the king of highly civilised Crete was turned by tradition into a murderous tyrant owning a monster and a labyrinth. It was the way of it in old France too, one thinks, when Charlemagne's height grew to eight feet, and his years were counted by centuries:—"He is three hundred years old, and when will he weary of war?" Anyhow, it has been the way of modern Ireland—the Ireland I know—and when I hear myth turned into history, or history into myth, I see in our stonebreakers and cattle drivers, the successors of Greek husbandmen or ancient vinedressers of the Loire.

I NOTICED some time ago, when listening to many legends of the Fianna, that it is about Finn, their leader, the most exaggerated of the tales have gathered; and I believe the reason is that he, being the greatest of the "Big Men," the heroic race, has been most often in the mouths of the people. They have talked of him by their firesides for two thousand years or so; at first earlier myths gathered around him, and then from time to time any unusual feats of skill or cunning shown off on one or other countryside, till many of the stories make him at the last grotesque, little more than a clown. So in Bible History, while lesser kings keep their dignity, great Solomon's wit is outwitted by the riddles of some countryman; and Lucifer himself, known in Kiltartan as "the proudest of the angels, thinking himself equal with God," has been seen in Sligo rolling down a road in the form of the *Irish Times*. The gods of ancient Ireland have not escaped. Mananaan, Son of the Sea, Rider of the Horses of the Sea, was turned long ago into a juggler doing tricks, and was hunted in the shape of a hare. Brigit, the "Fiery Arrow," the nurse of poets, later a saint and the Foster-mother of Christ, does her healing of the poor in the blessed wells of to-day as "a very civil little fish, very pleasant, wagging its tail."

GIOBNIU, the divine smith of the old times, made a new sword and a new spear for every one that was broken in the great battle between the gods and the mis-shapen Fomor. "No spearpoint that is made by my hand," he said, "will ever miss its mark; no man it touches will ever taste life again." It was his father who, with a cast of a hatchet, could stop the inflowing of the tide; and it was he himself whose ale gave lasting youth: "No sickness or wasting ever comes on those who drink at Giobniu's Feast." Later he became a saint, a master builder, builder of a house "more shining than a garden; with its stars, with its sun, with its moon." To-day he is known as the builder of the round towers of the early Christian centuries, and of the square castles of the Anglo-Normans. And the stories I have given of him, called as he now is, "the Goban Saor," show that he has fallen still farther in legend from his high origin.

As to O'Connell, perhaps because his name, like that of Finn and the Goban, is much in the mouths of the people, there is something of the grotesque already coming into his legend. The stories of him show more than any others how swiftly myths and traditions already in the air may gather around a memory much loved and much spoken of. I have known many who had seen and heard him speak, and yet he has already been given a miraculous birth, and the power of a saint is on its way to him. I would like those who come after me to keep their ears open to the growth of legend about him who was once my husband's friendly enemy, and afterwards his honoured friend.

I DO not take the credit or the discredit of the opinions given by the various speakers, nor do I go bail for the facts; I do but record what is already in "the Book of the People." The history of England and Ireland was shut out of the schools and it became a passion. As to why it was shut out, well, I heard someone whisper "Eugene Aram hid the body away, being no way anxious his scholars should get a sight of it." But this also was said in the barony of Kiltartan.

I HAVE added to the book a few of the ballads printed on broadsheets and sung at fairs or markets, that have to do with the English wars in which so many of our people have fought. I give also some that are concerned with the desire and attempt to break away from English rule. And if these are far from having the wildness and beauty of the passionate outcries made in earlier years in the native language, they are as I have called them elsewhere "roughly hammered links in a chain of unequal workmanship" that stretches back to the time when Spenser advised Queen Elizabeth to harry the poets out of Ireland.

A. GREGORY

COOLE, *February, 1926.*

THE KILTARTAN WONDER BOOK

THE MULE

WELL, I will tell you the story of a Mule was in the world one time, says the old man who had promised me a codfish and had only brought me a hake.

There were three sons of a King that had died, and they were living together, and there was a stable and a bird, and one of the sons was a bit simple. The bird used to be coming to the stable every morning and to be singing sweetly, and they all three fell in love with it and used to be trying to take it, but they could not. But one day the one that was a bit simple, that they called the Fool, took the tail off it. The bird said to him then: "You must follow me now until you find me"; and it went away, and he went following after it. And when he was on the height it was in the hollow, and when he was in the hollow it was on the height, and he never could come up with it; and at last it went out of his sight.

He came then to a wall, and he made a leap over it, and where did he come down but spread-legs on the back of a Mule that was in the field. "Are you a good jock?" says the Mule. "I am middling good," says he. "Hold on so," says the Mule, "and I will bring you to the place where the bird is." There was a wall in front of them—a double wall—and the Mule faced it, and went over it with one leap, and the Fool on his back. "You are the best jock ever I saw," says the Mule. "You are the best Mule ever I saw," says the Fool. They went on then as far as they could through the course of the day, till the Mule said: "I'm hungry now; go get me a few grains of oats." "How can I do that," says the Fool, "when I have no money?" "Go in there to that inn and get it for me, as I told you," says the Mule. "How much will do you?" says he. "Seven stone," says the Mule. So they stopped at the inn, and the Fool put him into the stable and bade the innkeeper to give him seven stone of oats. "Go in now and get your own dinner," says the Mule. So he went in and he got his dinner; and when he was ready to go, the innkeeper asked for the money. "I have none," says he. "Well I will keep the Mule in the stable till such time as you can pay me," says the innkeeper, and he went out and was going to lock the stable door, and the Mule gave a kick that broke his leg, and there he was lying on the ground. "Come on now," says the Mule; and the Fool got up on his back, and away with them again, and they came to a wall that was five miles in height. "At it now," says the Fool, and the Mule faced at it and crossed it with one leap. "You are a jock that can't be beat," says the Mule. "You are a Mule that can't be beat," says the Fool.

There was before them a lake that was five miles in length and five miles in breadth. "I am thirsty now," says the Mule, "after that feed I had. And I'll stop now till I'll take a drink," he says. "Do not," says the Fool, "or you will be heavy and not able to go." "Wait till you see that," says the Mule. So he stopped and he began to drink, and he never stopped till he had drunk up the whole of the lake that was five miles in length and five miles in breadth. They went on again till they came to a mountain that was before them, and the whole of the mountain was in one blaze, and there was a high wall before it, fifteen feet high. "Hold on now," says the Mule. "Here, at it," says the Fool, and the Mule crossed it with one leap; and when he came where the blaze was, he let out of his mouth all the water of the lake he had swallowed, and it quenched the blaze, and there they saw before them the bird. But if they did it went under ground, and the Mule followed it under ground into the enchanted place where it lived; and when they got there, it was not a bird, but the finest young lady that could be seen, and a King's daughter. The Fool asked her then to come along with him till he would marry her. "I will not," she said, "until such time as you will find my father, that I have hidden away from you." So he brought the Mule out to the stable, and he didn't know where to go look for the King. And when they were in the stable the Mule said: "The young lady has a hen clutching, and the place where it is clutching is in her own room under her bed. And under it you will find eleven eggs," he said, "and one of them is yellow and spotted. And take that one in your hand, and be going to smash it against the floor, and the King that is inside of it will cry out and will ask you to spare his life." So he went looking for the hen, and all happened as the Mule had said. "Will you marry me now?" says he to the young lady. "I will not," says she, "till you find my father that I have hidden a second time." So the place where she hid her father that time was in a duck's bill, and she put the duck out swimming in the middle of a pond. The young man went then to the stable and asked the Mule did he know where the King was hidden, and the Mule told him it was in the duck's bill. "And look at my tail," he said, "and see is there e'er a grey rib in it." So he looked, and there was a grey rib. "Pull it out," says the Mule, "and bring it to the pond where the duck is, and throw it out over the water, and however far the duck is, that rib will bring it back to the land. And catch a hold of it then, and threaten to cut the neck of it, and the King will cry out from its bill and ask you to spare him." So he did all that, and he spared the King, and then he went to the King's daughter. "Will you marry me this time?" says he. "I will not," says she, "till you find my father the third time." The place she hid him the third time was in a block of wood, and the Mule said to the young man: "Take a nail out from my shoe and drive it into the block of wood till you will split it." So he drew the nail, and he put it on the block of wood, and was going to split it, and the King called out for mercy, and he spared him.

After that he married the young lady, and himself and herself and the old King lived together, and there never were three people happier. And the Mule said: "Where will I go now?" "Go back," says the Fool, "to your own place, for you know the way well to it. But come back here at the end of seven years," he said, "till you'll see how am I getting on." So at the end of the seven years the Mule came back, and he asked to be taken into service. "I will never make a servant of you," says the Fool, "when I remember all the things you did for me, and all you helped me." "If that is so," says the Mule, "go and root up that little bush you see beyond, and give me three blows with the stump of it." So he did that, and with the three blows of the bush the enchantment went from the Mule, and who was he but the young man's own father, the King that was thought to be dead. So they all four lived together then and ever since, and the time I saw them myself they were well and happy and having great riches.

BESWARRAGAL

I WILL tell you the story of Beswarragal, said the old man of a hundred years old.

There was a King of Ireland out walking one time with his Grand Adviser. And they came to the side of a pool, and they saw in it a wild duck with a flock of twelve young ones, and she was pushing and beating away one of the young ones to make it leave the flock. "I wonder why is it the bird is doing that?" said the King. "It is the right thing, whenever there is a family of twelve, to send one of them away to seek a fortune for himself," says the Grand Adviser. "If that is so," says the King, "what way can I know which one of my sons must I send away?" "I will tell you that," says the Grand Adviser. "Let you watch them tomorrow the time they are coming home from the school, and close the gate on whichever one of them will be last, and let him be the one you will send away." So the next day they watched the twelve sons coming from the school, and the one that was last at the gate was the youngest of them all. "Oh, give him another chance," says the King. So the next day they watched again, and it was the same one, the youngest, that was last at the gate; and the third day it was the same thing. "Oh," says the King, "it is worse to me the youngest to go than any two of the others." "You need not mind that," says the Grand Adviser, "for I can tell you that the life he will have will be a happy one." "I am content so," says the King.

So the King sent for him then, and he gave him a purse of money that would last him for ten years or for twenty years, and he bade him go make a way for himself.

So the King's son set out, and he travelled the roads till night time, and he saw a cottage before him, and a light in it, and he opened the door and went in, and all he saw in it was one old man. "A welcome before you, King's son," says the old man. "I thank you for that welcome," says he; "but how is it you know me to be a King's son?" So the old man showed him a sword that hung over the top of the door. "If any man comes through that door," he says, "that is not a King's son, that sword will fall and will whip the head off him. And it is a good time you came here," he said, "and you could have come at no better time." "Why is that?" says the young man. "There is a pool there beyond," says the old man, "and one morning in the whole year, there comes to it

Beswarragal, that is the most beautiful woman of the whole world, having her twelve waiting maids with her, and they go swimming in that pool. And to-morrow is the day they are coming," he said, "and let you hide yourself till they will go into the water, and Beswarragal will be the last to strip, and let you take her clothes and hide them, and she will not be able to go away, and whatever you will ask her she will do it. And what you will ask of her is herself," he said.

So the young man went down to the pool, and Beswarragal and her twelve beautiful waiting maids were in the water, and he took her clothes and hid them. And when they were tired swimming they put their clothes on, and then they turned to birds and they flew away, all but Beswarragal, and she could not fly. So the King's son came to her and he gave her the clothes. "What will you give me now?" says he. "I will give you anything you will ask," says she. "I ask nothing but yourself," says he; "you to marry me and to be my wife." "How will you go away with me and you not able to fly?" says she. But she put a loop of the chain she had about his neck, and she took him by the hand and she flew away with him to a garden, and she brought him into the gardener's house. "And there is one thing I have to tell you," said she; "you must never wonder at me or say anything about me at all." "I will never do that," says he. And every day she brought him food to the gardener's house, and they lived together there for a while.

(The old man of a hundred years was getting tired, and the old woman that was his wife sent out the old woman sitting on the doorstep to get him a glass of porter. The old man drank a sup of it, and then the story went on.)

But at last one day she passed by him in the garden, and when he saw her so beautiful he turned and he said to the gardener: "There was never a lady so beautiful as mine in the whole world." "There never was," says the gardener. "And you will be without her now," he says.

So the next morning Beswarragal brought him his breakfast, and, "Oh," she said, "why did you speak of me and wonder at me, for I must go away from you now to Righ-na-Sluagh, and you will never see me again." "How could I help wondering at you," he said, "and you so beautiful passing by? And I will go following after you for ever," he said.

So she went away, and before she went she left five drops of honey on his five fingers. And he left the garden and went following after and looking for her in every place.

He walked on all through the day, and at the fall of night he cane to a house that had but an old man in it. "God be with the company left me to-day," says he. "What company was that?" says the King's son. "Beswarragal and her twelve young girls," says he. "That is the one I am looking for," says the King's son. "You never will get her," says the old man. "But I will do this for you," he says; "I will give you a ball when you leave this to-morrow, and you can go throwing it before you, and if you can come up with it as fast as it goes, you will come to my brother and he might help you."

So after breakfast he took the ball, and he went throwing it and following it through the day till he came to a house where the old man's brother was, and he went in. "God be with the company that left me to-day—that was Beswarragal and her twelve young ladies," says the old man. "She is the one I am looking for," says the King's son. "You never will get up to her," says the old man; "but I will do this for you," he says. "There are twelve horses in the stable outside; and go into it," he says, "and take down the bridle you will see behind the stable door, and shake it, and whatever horse will come and put its head in it, let you get up on it, and it will bring you on the road she is gone." So after breakfast in the morning he went out into the stable and got the bridle and shook it, and a little *gioblacan* of an Arabian horse came running and put his head into it. "The devil's welcome to you," says he, "and all the good horses there are in the stable!" "He'll answer you well," says the old man, "and get up on him now. And are you a good jock ?" he says. "I am," says the King's son, and he got up on it. "Let you leap that now," says the old man, and he turned the horse to where there was a big estate-wall at the side of the place. "It is humbugging you are," says the King's son, "for there is no one would be able to leap that wall." But the little Arabian of a horse rose off the ground, and made the wild cat's bow in the air, and he came down the other side of the wall, but the King's son fell on the ground. But he rose up again and got up on the little horse. "We will make a start now," he says. "You will never get to the place where Beswarragal is," says the old man, "for there is a place between this and it, and the birds that fly high in the air fall down in ashes passing over that place, with all the fire that is blazing up a mile high from it, and that is thrown up out of it."

The pony set out then, and the King's son on his back, and away with them till they came in sight of the fiery place. "Put your hand in my ear," says the pony, "and take out a bottle that is in it, and you will find food for yourself and white-water for myself in it." So he took the bottle and he gave white-water to the horse, and he rubbed what was in the bottle to its hoofs, and it made a great leap into the air and over the fiery place, and pitched five miles on the other side, and nothing harmed but that the hair was burned off its belly.

And where they pitched there was a little house, and an old woman in it, and she gave them shelter for the night. And in the night seven men came in, and some having but half a head and some with their hands and their arms cut off them. "Who are those and what happened them?" said the King's son. "They are my own sons," says the old woman, "and every night through seven years there are men coming in boats and fighting them, and that leave them that way. And all they kill of them are alive again in the morning," she said, "and they themselves will be healed again in the morning as well as before." "I will go and kill them," says the King's son. So he went down to the boats and drove away the men.

Then he went on to a house that was within a quarter of a mile of the house where Beswarragal was, and he asked lodging. "Why would you come in here," says the man of the house, "and why wouldn't you go where everyone is going—to that big house beyond, where the wedding is going to be?" So he asked for a cook's suit, and he put it on him, and he went on to Beswarragal's house, and there were hundreds and hundreds going into it for her wedding. "Are you wanting a cook?" says the King's son at the door. "He was never more wanted," said they, "and if there were ten of them they would be welcome."

So they sent him to the kitchen, and he asked the head cook for flour and things to mix a cake, and he mixed it; and when he had made ready to bake he put the print of his five fingers on the top of it, and put it in the oven. And when it was baked he put a cover over it and gave it to the servants that were bringing up the dinner, and he said: "Give that cake to Beswarragal and to no other one."

So it was put before her on the table, and she took it to eat a bit of it; and when she tasted it, and that she broke it and saw the five drops of honey in it, she said: "Where is the man that made that cake? And wherever he is send him up to me," she said. For she had found the five drops of honey inside the cake.

So they went to him, and he asked leave to change his cook's suit, and they gave him that. And he came up and Beswarragal knew him, and she put her arms about him. And the man that was to be her husband, he jumped out of the window and broke his skull on the pavement.

So the King's son and Beswarragal went away back to the garden; but it wasn't long till a man came that had wings and could fly, and he stooped down and took up Beswarragal, as if she was a child, and brought her away. The King's son went following her then, and he went on till he came to the man that had wings, and he asked her of him. "There was a man came that could not fly, but that was a better man than myself," says he, "and he took her from me." So the King's son went on till he found that man, and he asked her of him. "There was a man came," he said, "that had seven colours in his eyes, and that took her from me," he said.

So he went on till he came to the man that had seven colours in his eyes and asked her of him. "She was brought away from me," says he, "by the Queen of the Black Wood. And there is no one will be able to take her out of her hands," he said.

So the King's son went on, and he had no knowledge what way to get to the Black Wood. And he was passing through a field, and a white *garran* that was in the field spoke to him and said: "Get up now on my back, and I will bring you as far as the stile that leads into the Black Wood. But there is no one can go into it," he said, "because it is as dark as night; and there is no one can face the strength of the Queen that is in that wood."

So the King's son got up on the *garran*, and they went on till they came to the road that was outside the Black Wood, and there was an old man there was building a castle on a very large flagstone, and he asked the King's son where was he going, and he said he was going to bring away his wife from the Queen of the Black Wood. "There is no one can do that," says the old man, "unless it is the man that will put this castle five yards off the flagstone, with one shove he will give it." So the King's son went at it, and he gave it one shove, and if he did he put the castle eight yards from the flagstone. "Oh," says the old man when he saw that, "I know you must be my sister's son, for there is no one in the whole world could do that unless my sister's son." And he put his arms about him and kissed him. And then he bade him to move the flagstone and he did that, and there was a sword under it. "Take up that sword," says the old man, "and be shaking it this way and that way. And according as you will be shaking it, the strength will be going out of the Queen of the Black Wood, and you can go to her when she is left weak," he said.

So the King's son did as he bade him, and by the time he came to the Queen, all he had to was to whip the head off her.

So he brought Beswarragal out of the wood, and they went back safe and well again to the garden.

"Is there any meaning in the name Beswarragal?"

"Not a meaning; it was all the name ever she had, and it will be her name ever and always."

HE CAME DOWN SPREAD LEGS ON A MULE.

THE KING WAS HID IN THE YELLOW EGG.

The old wife of the man of a hundred years, who had fallen asleep listening, says to the old woman who was sitting on the doorstep. "Would you say was there any meaning in the name?" And she says, "I suppose she was just an enchanted woman." "Ah," says the old man, "I'll give you three words that will bring you to Heaven as easy as walking out into that street. And I will tell you now about the Seven Fishers."

THE SEVEN FISHERS

THERE were Seven Fishers went out one time from Galway, and a strange sort of a wind blew one of the seven a long way off out into the sea. And when the fisherman came back, he went up to the house and he called to his daughter and he said: "I have but the one fish, but let you clean it and bring it to the shop, and it will get us our supper."

So she brought it out of the boat, and she was cleaning it and rubbing it, and while she was doing that it turned to be a tall fine man standing before her. And he stopped with her for a while, and when he was going away he said: "You will have two sons, and you will never know want, and your father will get fish every time he will go out. And here is a letter," he said, "and give it to the sons at whatever time they will ask tidings of their father."

So all happened as he said, and she brought up the sons and reared them, and at the last she sent them to get learning in Dublin. And when they got there they saw ball-playing going on, and there was a dispute, and those that were disputing called out to the young men to settle it, and they gave their opinion. "Ah," said the ball-players then, "who are those that are giving a judgment? Scamps that don't know who is their father."

Then the young men looked one at another. "That is true," they said, "and we have no business here, but let us go home again." So they turned and went back, and when they came to Galway there was a hurling, and a gentleman that was at the head of one side came to them and said: "Two of my own men have failed me, and come you take their place at the hurling." "We never played it, and we know nothing of it," said they. "No matter," says he; "come and stand up now." So they stood up, and when the ball came near them, the one of them made a leap and struck it, and the other got the goal. And when they were leaving the field they heard the people saying to one another: "It is the Fish's sons were the best."

They looked at one another then, and they went home and asked the mother was she their own mother. "I am that," says she. Then they asked news of their father, and she gave them the letter he had left with her. And it gave directions to the eldest son to go to such a cliff, and he would find a flagstone with a keyhole and a key, and it bade him turn the key and take out what he would find in it.

So he went to the cliff and he opened the flagstone, and under it he found a good suit and a horse, and he put on the suit and he got on the horse. "How long will you stop on me?" says the horse. "As long as the saddle is under me," says he. "That is not enough," says the horse. "Well, as long as the skin is left on you," says he. "That will do," says the horse. So he set out then till he came to the Court of the King of Munster, that had never spoken a word and never made a laugh for seven years.

The Fish's son went in and he asked the King why was he seven years without speaking a word. "It is my daughter that was brought away from me," says he, "by Croagcill, that beat me in a battle, and that no man can beat; for he has the strength of a man in every rib of his hair." "I will go bring her back to you," says the Fish's son.

So they made ready a cake for him, and away with him till he met with an old man, and he asked him did he know where was Croagcill living. "I never came to the place where he is living," said the old man, "and I have been walking for the last four hundred years."

The Fish's son went on then till he came to a wood and he met with a white hound, and she searching after food. "It is hungry you are," says the Fish's son. "I am not," says the hound, "but the young ones I have are hungry." So he gave her then the half of the cake, and she was very thankful, and she said she would come to his help at any time he would be in need of her, and he to give a call for her, or a whistle. He went on then till he came to the strand, and he sat down to eat the half of the cake he had left, and there came a hawk and asked a share of it, and he gave her a share. "Can you give me any tidings of Croagcill and of where he is living?" says he to the hawk. "I went as far as Croagcill once," says the hawk; "and I will give you a little canoe of a boat," says she, "will bring you to him. But it will be hard for you to kill him," says she, "for there is no one knows where his body is or where he has it hid. And call to me if I can give help to you," says she, "and any good anyone can do for you I'll do it."

So he went in the boat, and it had charms in it, that it brought him as far as Croagcill's house. The King's daughter saw him coming, and she ran out to meet him. "My thousand welcomes to you," says she, "for I thought I never would see one of Ireland's men again." So he told her he had come to bring her back to her father in Munster. "Oh, what can I do with you now," says she; "for when Croagcill comes home he will kill you?"

She put him in hiding before evening in a box, and Croagcill came in, and having a heavy deer upon his shoulders. He drew it through the fire, and through the ashes, and through his long, cold teeth, and there was not one bit left but the bones. "Fru, fra, feasog," he says then; "I feel the smell of a sweet-voiced liar of an Irishman in some place that is not far off." "My dear and my love, and my man that is better than his father," says the King's daughter, "it is that I myself was at the top of the house, and there came a little bird from Ireland and perched upon my hand." "Maybe so, maybe so," says he. "You to get your death," says the King's daughter; "what at all would I do being left in this strange house?" "Och," says he, "I will never get my death; for there is no one knows where the life of my body is hid." "Oh, and where is it?" says the King's daughter. "It is in the green plot that is outside the door," says he.

He went out in the morning, and the King's daughter rose up and she took roses and posies and every sort that was pretty, and she put them out on the green plot. And she let the Fish's son come out for the daytime, and she put him back in the box at night. When Croagcill drew to the house in the evening there was a big beast upon his shoulders, and he drew it through the fire, and through the ashes, and through his long, cold teeth, and there was not a bit left on it. "Fru, fra, feasog, I get the smell of the sweet-voiced, lying Irishman coming to my house to-night," says he. "My love and my secret, there is nothing at all but what it used to be in it," says she. "There is, and more," says he. "Oh, I was up at the top of the castle, and a little bird from Ireland came and perched on my head," says she. "Maybe so, maybe so," says Croagcill. He went out then. "What is the reason the green plot to be full of roses and posies?" says he. "Didn't I hear you say," says she, "that is the place your life is?" "Och," says he, "you to know the place where my life is, it is likely you would have affection for it." "I would indeed be fond of it," says she. "Well," says he, "there is a green holly-bush beyond at the brink of the sea, and it is inside that tree my life is, and I will never get my death till the Fish's son from Ireland will come and will cut down that tree with his sword, and that is a thing will not happen for ever."

In the morning Croagcill went out to the wood, and the Fish's son took his sword and began to cut the holly-tree. And when he had it near cut through, the red fox ran out from the roots, and it is in that fox Croagcill's life was. Then the Fish's son gave a call and a whistle, and the white hound from the wood came and followed after the fox, and they were going up and down and there and hither in every part, and at the last the hound got a grip of the fox. But with that it changed into a bird and went flying up high over the tide. "Oh, where is now the grey hawk of the dark earth?" says the Fish's son. So the hawk was there on the minute, and she made a dart at the bird in the air, and caught it in her claws and killed it that it dropped into the sea, and at that minute Croagcill dropped dead where he was, and there was an end of him.

They gathered all he had of riches, and they went back to the King of Munster's house. The King was very glad to see them coming home. "You can take my daughter now," says the King, "and you can join and be married to one another." So they married and wedded together, and there was a wedding feast for a year and a day for them, and it was as good the last day as at the first.

SHAWNEEN

THERE was a King one time was very much put out because he had no son, and he went at last to consult his Chief Adviser. And the Chief Adviser said: "It is easy enough managed if you do as I tell you. Let you send some one," says he, "to such a place to catch a fish. And when the fish is brought in, give it to the Queen, your wife, to eat."

So the King sent as he was bade, and the fish was caught and brought in, and he gave it to the cook, and bade her put it before the fire, but to be careful with it, and not to let any blob or blister rise on it. But it is impossible to cook a fish before the fire without the skin of it rising in some place or other, and so there came a blob on the skin, and the cook put her finger on it to smooth it down, and then she put her finger into her mouth to cool it, and so she got a taste of the fish. And then it was sent up to the Queen, and she ate it, and what was left of it was thrown out into the yard, and there was a mare in the yard, and a greyhound, and they ate the bits that were thrown out.

And before a year was out the Queen had a young son, and the cook had a young son, and the mare had two foals, and the greyhound had two pups.

And the two young men were sent off for a while to some place to be cared, and when they came back they were so much like one another no person could say which was the Queen's son and which was the cook's. And the Queen was vexed at that, and she went to the Chief Adviser and said: "Tell me some way that I can know which is my own son, for I don't like to be giving the same eating and drinking to the cook's son as to my own." "It is easy to know that," said the Chief Adviser, "if you will do as I tell you. Go you outside, and stand at the door they will be coming in by, and when they see you, your own son will bow his head, but the cook's son will only laugh."

So she did that, and when her own son bowed his head her servants put a mark on him, that she would know him again. And when they were all sitting at their dinner after that, she said to Shawneen, that was the cook's son: "It is time for you to go away out of this, for you are not my son." And her own son, that we will call Shamus, said: "Do not send him away; are we not brothers?" But Shawneen said: "I would have been long ago out of this house if I knew it was not my own father and mother owned it." And for all Shamus could say to him, he would not stop. But before he went they were by the well that was in the garden, and he said to Shamus: "If harm ever happens to me, that water on the top of the well will be blood, and the water below will be honey."

Then he took one of the pups, and one of the two horses that was foaled after the mare eating the fish, and the wind that was after him could not catch him, and he caught the wind that was before him. And he went on till he came to a cooper's house, and he asked did he want a servant. "Well," says the cooper, "I have thirteen goats—twelve goats and a puck—and let you bring them out and be minding them to-morrow." "I will do that for you," says Shawneen. So the cooper engaged him, and on the morrow he brought out the goats to the place he was bade, that was the top of a mountain. And there was a gentleman's demesne, and walls about it, and he looked in at the gate and he saw grass growing up as high as the trees. "Why wouldn't my poor goats go in there," says he, "and be grazing in it, and not to be out on that red mountain where there is not a rib of grass, and what they are eating is clay?" So he drove in the goats through the gate, and they were eating the grass, and he heard some person coming, and he went up in a tree. He saw a giant coming into the field. The giant looked at him. "I see where you are in the tree," says he. "And I think you too big for one mouthful," says he; "and I think you too small for two mouthfuls, and I don't know what will I do with you unless I will grind you up and make snuff for my nose." "As you are strong be merciful," says Shawneen up in the tree. "Come down out of that, you little dwarf," says the giant, "or I'll tear you and the tree asunder." So Shawneen came down. "Would you sooner be driving red-hot knives into one another's hearts," says the giant, "or would you sooner be fighting one another on red-hot flags?" "Fighting on red-hot flags is what I'm used to at home," says Shawneen; "and your dirty feet will be sinking in them and my feet will be rising." So then they began the fight. The ground that was hard they made soft, and the ground that was soft they made hard, and they made spring-wells come up through the green flags. They were like that all through the day, no one getting the upper hand of the other; and at last a little bird came and sat on the bush and said to Shawneen: "If you won't make an end of him by sunset, he'll make an end of you." Then Shawneen put out his strength, and he brought the giant down on his knees. "Give me my life," says the giant, "and I'll give you the best gift I have." "What gift is that?" says Shawneen. "A Sword that nothing can stand against," says the giant. "Where is it to be found?" says Shawneen. "In that red door you see there in the hill." So Shawneen went and got it out. "Where will I try the Sword?" says he. "Try it on that ugly black stump of a tree," says the giant. "I see nothing blacker or uglier than your own head," says Shawneen. And with that he made one stroke, and cut off the giant's head that it went into the air, and he caught it on the Sword as it was coming down, and made two halves of it. "It is well for you I did not join to the body again," says the head, "or you would never have been able to strike it off again." "I did not give you the chance of that," says Shawneen. And he brought away the great Sword with him.

So he brought the goats home at evening, and everybody wondered at all the milk they gave that night. And when the cooper was eating his supper he said: "I think I only hear two roars from beyond to-night, in place of three."

The next morning Shawneen went out again with the goats, and he saw another demesne with good grass in it, and he brought in the goats. All happened the same as the first day, but the giant that came this time had two heads, and they fought together, and the little bird came and spoke to Shawneen as before. And when the giant was brought down by Shawneen he said: "Give me my life and I will give you the best thing I have." "What thing is that?" says Shawneen. "It is a Cloak of Darkness you can put on, and you will see everyone but no one can see you." "Where is it?" says Shawneen. "It's inside that little red door at the side of the hill." So Shawneen went and brought out the Cloak. And then he cut off the giant's two heads, and caught them coming down, and made four halves of them. And they said it was well for him he had not given them time to join the body.

That night when the goats came home all the vessels that could be found were filled up with milk.

The next morning Shawneen went out again, and all happened as before, and the giant this time had four heads, and Shawneen made eight halves of them. And the giant told him to go to a little blue door in the side of the hill, and there he got a pair of Shoes of Swiftness, that when you put them on would make you run faster than the wind.

That night the goats gave so much milk there was no place to hold it. "Oh, what can we do for vessels to hold the milk?" says the cooper, and they were milking the poor goats on the ground, and it was given to poor people and men passing the road. I was passing that way myself, and I got a drink of it. "Why is it," says the cooper, "the goats are giving so much milk these days? Are you bringing them to any other grass?" "I am not," says Shawneen, "but I have a good stick, and whenever they would stop still or lie down I give them blows of it, that they jump over walls and stones and ditches; that's the way to make them give plenty of milk." And that night at supper the cooper said: "I hear no roars at all."

The next day Shawneen brought the goats to the first meadow he went to, and there came before him the mother of the three giants, that was the strongest of them all. "Was it you killed my three sons?" says she. "It was," says Shawneen. "I thought," says she, "the man wasn't born in Ireland that could do that much." So they took a hold of one another and went wrestling, and neither of them got the better of the other through the length of the day. And it is the way it was, the two farthest back teeth in the mother's mouth were crutches to her, that reached down to the ground, the way Shawneen would not get a good grip of her at one side or the other. And at the fall of day the little bird came and sat on the bush and said: "Why wouldn't you give a tip to the crutch?" So with that he gave a tip of his boot to the tooth, that knocked it out of her head, and the mother fell, and before she died she gave him up her estate.

Shawneen left the cooper's house then, and he went on till he came to a large garden, and he went up in the branches of a cherry-tree, and he was eating the cherries and throwing the stones down. There came in a young lady, and she looked up and she saw him in the tree. "Oh, you are an unruly lad," says she, "for that tree belongs to the King that is my father, and what right have you to go plundering it down?" So he came down then out of the tree, and he asked what could he do for her. "Go out and bring me news," says she, "is the Black Duke coming to make a good fight against the Fiery Dragon." The Fiery Dragon now was a fish that used to come every seven years, and he should get the primest lady in the land to eat and to banish. And it was the King's daughter was to be given to him on that very day, unless the Black Duke or some other champion would get the better of him. And it was given out that whatever man would kill the Dragon would get the King's daughter for his wife.

So Shawneen went down by the road to the sea, and he came to a cluster of brambles and of bushes that was beside the road, and he looked in, and who was hiding in it but the Black Duke. "Why wouldn't you go fight?" says Shawneen; "and thousands of people and carriages there looking on." "Oh, I am in dread," says the Black Duke; for he was a great coward, and he was afeared to go on and to face the Fiery Dragon. "Give me here your suit of armour," says Shawneen. So he got the suit of armour and he went on to the brink of the sea, and it was like the Cliffs of Moher; all the people were looking down from it, and there on the strand the King's daughter was sitting and she crying, and tied in a silver chair. And she saw Shawneen coming, and he wearing the Black Duke's suit. "Let me lie a while with my head on your knee," says he, "and you can waken me when the Dragon is coming." So he did that, and she saw the Fiery Dragon coming, and its mouth open and a fiery flame from it, and nine miles of the sea was dry with all he drank of it. So she wakened Shawneen, and they had a great fight, and he got the better of the Fiery Dragon. "Oh, let me go out of this for the night," says the Dragon, "and I'll come back in the early morning out of the salt sea." So Shawneen let him go, and as to himself, he put on the Shoes of Swiftness that no one would overtake him, and he went back to the cooper's house for the night.

Well, the next day he came again, and there was no news or tidings of the Black Duke, and all happened as before, and he drove back the Fiery Dragon till the next morning.

And the third day Shawneen came again and he lay down to take a sleep while he was waiting, with his head in the lap of the King's daughter. And this time she thought some way he was maybe not the Black Duke, and she took her scissors and cut off a bunch of his hair. "Are you cutting all the hair off my head?" says he. "I am cutting it," says she, "till I'll know who was it made an end of the Fiery Dragon." So she made a little packet of it and put it away, and, another thing she drew off a golden shoe from his foot. And when she saw the Dragon coming she awoke him, and he said: "This time I will put the Dragon in a way he will eat no more king's daughters." So he took out the Sword he had got from the giant, and he drove the Dragon to his knees out in the sea, and down to the hip, and gave him a blow that split him in two halves from the head to the tail, and there was an end of him. And he put on the Cloak of Darkness he had taken from the giant, that no one saw what way did he go, and away with him to the cooper's house.

Then the King made ready the wedding, and he sent for the Black Duke that was to marry his daughter, and he was made much of and was the right-hand man, and there was music and shouting before him, and the greatest wedding given out that ever was. But the King's daughter knew well it was not the Black Duke had saved her, and she took out the bunch of hair she had, and she said she would marry no one but the man whose hair would match that; and she showed the gold shoe and said she would marry no one but the man whose foot would fit it. And the Black Duke tried to

put on the shoe, but so much as his toe would not go into it; and
as for his hair, it did not match at all to the bunch of hair she had
cut from the man that saved her.

So then the King gave a great ball to bring all the chief men of
the country together, to try would the shoe fit any of them. And
they were all going to carpenters and joiners getting bits of their
feet cut off to try could they wear the shoe, but it was no use; not
one of them could get it on. Then the King went to his Chief
Adviser and asked what could he do. And the Chief Adviser bade
him to give another ball. "And this time," he said, "give it to poor
as well as rich."

So the ball was given and many came flocking to it, but the shoe
would not fit any one of them. And there were two Fools passing the
way and they said: "There is a wedding going on, the greatest
that ever was in the world; and let us go in now," they said, "and
we will be eating meat." So they went in and sat by the kitchen
fire, and the King asked had everyone in the house or out of the
house tried to see would the bunch of hair fit to their poll, and they
said all unless the two Fools that were sitting by the kitchen fire.
So they were brought up and bade to take their caps off, but the
hair did not match their own. And the Chief Adviser said: "Is
everyone here belonging to the district?" "They are all here,"
said the King, "unless the boy that minds the cooper's goats. And
I would not like him to be coming up here," he said. So Shawneen
was sent for, and he was told what the King said, and that vexed
him, where he knew the two Fools had got their chance. And he
got his sword and came running up the stairs as if to strike off the
King's head. But when he got to the top of the stairs the King's
daughter saw him and she gave a cry and ran into his arms. And
they tried the shoe and it fitted him, and his hair matched to the
bunch that had been cut off. That was a good thought the King's
daughter had to cut a bit of his hair; and there is nothing in the
world so quick as a woman's thought. A man's thought is quick
enough, but a woman's thought is quicker again.

And Shawneen took the Black Duke and bound him with gads,
that no one would be able to loosen but himself, and everyone was
striving to loosen the gads, but they could not: and Shawneen was
bade come and try his hand at them, but he said he would not till
the Royal Family themselves would come asking him. So they
came, and the gads loosened of themselves, and Shawneen and
the King's daughter were married; and a great feast was given for
three days and three nights, and there was every sort of fiddlers
and of pipers at the wedding.

And at the end of that time, one morning there came a deer outside the window, with bells on it, and they ringing. And it called out: "Here is the hunt; where are the huntsman and the hounds?" So when Shawneen heard that, he got up and took his horse and his hound and went hunting the deer. When it was in the hollow he was on the hill, and when it was on the hill he was in the hollow; and that went on all through the day, and when night fell it went into a wood. And Shawneen went into the wood after it, and all he could see was a mud-wall cabin, and he went in, and there he saw an old woman, about two hundred years old, and she sitting over the fire. "Did you see a deer pass this way?" says Shawneen. "I did not," says she. "But it's too late for you to be following a deer; let you stop here the night." "What will I do with my horse and hound?" says Shawneen. "Here are two ribs of hair," says she, "and let you tie them up with those ribs." So Shawneen went out and tied up the horse and the hound, and when he came in again the old woman said: "It was you killed my three grandsons," she said, "and I'm going to kill you now." And she put on a pair of boxing gloves, each one of them nine stone weight, and the nails in them fifteen inches long. Then they began to fight, and Shawneen was getting the worst of it. "Help, hound!" he cried out then. "Squeeze, hair!" called out the old woman, and the rib of hair that was around the hound's neck squeezed him to death. "Help, horse!" cried Shawneen. "Squeeze hair!" screeched out the hag, and the rib of hair that was about the horse's neck began to tighten and to squeeze him to death. Then the old woman made an end of Shawneen, and threw him outside the door.

To go back now to Shamus. He was out in the garden one day, and he took a look at the well, and what did he see but that the water at the top was blood, and what was underneath was honey. So he went into the house again, and he said to his mother: "I will never eat a second meal at the same table, or sleep a second night in the same bed, till I know what is happening to Shawneen."

So he took the other horse then and the hound, and he set off over hills where cock never crows and wind never blows, and the old boy himself never sounds his horn. And at last he came to the cooper's house, and when he came in the cooper said: "You are welcome, and I can give you better treatment than I did the last time you came in to me;" for he thought it was Shawneen was in it, they were so much like one another. "That is good," says Shamus to himself. "My brother has been in this place." And he gave the cooper the full of a basin of gold in the morning before he left the place.

Then he went on till he came to the King's house, and when he was at the door the King's daughter came running down the stairs. "Oh, you are welcome back to me!" says she, for she thought it was Shawneen, her husband, was in it. And all the people said: "It is a wonder you to have gone hunting three days after your marriage, and to stop so long away."

Well, the next morning the deer came, and bells ringing on her, under the windows, and called out: "The hunt is here; where are the huntsman and the hounds?" Then Shamus got up and took his horse and his hound, and followed her over hills and hollows till they came to the wood, and there he saw nothing but the mud-wall cabin, and the old woman sitting by the fire, and she bade him stop the night there, and gave him two ribs of hair to tie up his horse and his hound. But Shamus was wittier than Shawneen, and before he went out he threw the ribs of hair into the fire secretly. When he came in the old woman said: "Your brother killed my three grandsons, and I killed him, and I'll kill you along with him." And she put her gloves on, and they began the fight, and then Shamus called out: "Help, horse!" "Squeeze, hair!" called out the hag. "I can't squeeze; I'm in the fire," says the hair. And the horse came in and gave her a blow of the hoof. "Help, hound!" says Shamus then. "Squeeze, hair!" says the hag. "I can't; I'm in the fire," says the second hair. Then the hound put his teeth in her, and Shamus brought her down, and she cried for mercy. "Give me my life," says she, "and I'll tell you where you'll get your brother again, and his hound and his horse." "Where is that?" says Shamus. "Do you see that rod over the fire?" says she. "Let you take it down and go outside the door, where you will see three green stones, and strike them with the rod, for they are your brother and his horse and his hound, and they will come to life again." "I will do that, but I will make a green stone of yourself first," says Shamus; and he cut off her head with his sword. Then he went out and struck the stones, and sure enough there was Shawneen and his horse and hound, alive and well. And they began striking other stones that were there, and the rod rose the charm from them, and men came out that had been turned to stones, hundreds and thousands of them.

Then they went home, and Shawneen and his wife lived happy ever after, and they had children by the basketful, and threw them out by the shovelful. I was passing one time myself, and they called me in and gave me a cup of tea.

THE MAN THAT SERVED THE SEA

I WILL tell you a story about a man that served the sea. It came to him first in a dream to do that, and he was for seven years serving it, going down by the sea every day. And at the last he saw a mermaid in the water, and she combing her head, and he made a grab at her and brought her to the house. And he took the cover off of her, that was the same as a tail, and she was the most beautiful young lady that ever was seen, and he married her. But he hid the cover up in the roof of the house, the way she would not see it, and think of the sea.

She was with him for seven years, and by the will of God they had three sons, and through all that time she never spoke a word, but she laughed three times. The first time she laughed was one day the dinner was on the fire in the pot, and a man that came in was sitting by the hearth, and they asked him would he eat a share of the victuals, and he gave a curse and he said: "Sorra bit will I eat." She gave a laugh when she heard that. The second time she laughed was one day the pot was on the fire and the dinner was boiling, and the husband's mother that was minding it did not take the top off. For it is the custom with our people to take the top off what is in the pot, and to throw it in behind the fire.

And the third time she laughed was one day the husband's mother was going into the parlour, and was knocked going in at the door.

Well, at the end of the seven years the cover fell down from the top of the house, and she got a little sketch of it, and she took it and tried it on. And with that she went out of the house into the sea, and brought the three sons along with her, and came back to the house no more.

And the man was going every day to the sea looking for her, and at last, at the end of nine years, he got a sketch of her where she was sitting on a rock, and he made a grab for her. But she said: "You have no chance of getting me at all, or of bringing me back to the house. But I'll do this for you," she said; "the eldest son I had, I'll give him back to you if you will promise to leave him all that you have. But as for myself, you will never see me again," she said. "Is it any harm to ask you," says the husband, "what was it made you laugh the first time in the house?" "I will tell you that," says she. "I laughed to hear that man make the curse, for when he did, all that was in the pot went to nothing." "And is it any harm to ask you why you laughed the second and the third time?" says the husband. "The second time I laughed," says she, "was when your mother didn't take the top off the pot. For all that was in it turned to poison then," says she, "and I took no taste of it myself. And the third time I laughed," she said, "was when your mother was knocked going in at the parlour door. For I saw what it was knocked her," she said. "It was the leg of a pot that was standing up out of the floor, and that was full of gold. And go home now," she said, "and dig under the threshold of the door, and you will find the pot of gold, and you can keep all that is in it."

So the man did that, and he brought his eldest son with him, and he dug under the floor and found the pot of gold, and they were very rich from that time.

That is all, my lady, I know about it; and that is one of the old stories of Ireland.

THE BULLOCKEEN

THERE was a King, and it is a good while ago he was in it, and he married a King's daughter, and at the end of two years they had a son, and the mother died. And before dying she made a will, and she willed to the son but one thing only—a little black Bullockeen was out in the meadow. And she laid commands on the King: "Do not marry another woman," she said, "till the son I have left with you will give you leave three times to do it."

And the son grew to be about seven years old, and he bought a hurling stick and a silver ball, and he used to go hurling. And one day he was putting the ball, and when he'd give it a blow that sent it over, he would be over before it would fall, and when he would strike it hither, he'd be hither before it, he was that smart, that it would not fall to the ground. The King was passing that way, and when he saw him he said: "It's a pity your mother not to see you," says he, "for it is proud out of you she would be this day." "Let you leave talking of my mother and let you take another woman," says the son.

Well, the next day he was out with the ball again, and he was twice smarter that day, and to throw the ball over, he would be over before it, and to hit it back hither, he would be hither before it, the way it didn't touch the ground at all through that day. The King was looking at him. "It's a pity your mother not to be here and to see you," says he. "It is time for you to put another woman's skin on my mother," says the son. And the same thing happened on the third day.

So he married another King's daughter, and the King's son had a step-mother, and a bad step-mother she was. She had three daughters, and she used to be starving the King's son, and not to be giving him nourishment; but he had nothing but hardship, and all she would give him to eat was stirabout, and she used to be giving all to the daughters.

He was out in the field one day, and the little black Bullockeen came to him and it said: "I know the way you are treated," it said, "and the sort of nourishment they are giving you. And unscrew now my left horn," it said, "and take what you will find out of it." So he unscrewed the left horn, and the first thing he took out was a napkin, and he spread it out on the grass; and then he took out cups and plates and every sort of food, and he sat down and ate

BESWARRAGAL AND THE MAN WITH WINGS.

BESWARRAGAL AND HER MAIDENS BATHE -

IT IS IN THAT FOX FROGGILL'S LIFE WAS.

A GENTLEMAN'S DEMESNE AND WALLS ABOUT IT.

and drank his enough. And then he put back the napkin and all into the horn again, and screwed it on.

That was going on every day, and he used to be throwing his stirabout away into the ash-bin; and the servants found it, and they told the Queen that he was throwing away what they gave him, and getting fat all the same. And the Queen did not know what to do, and she would give the whole world to get quit of him, he being so smart; but she could get no way to do it.

So she sent for an old prophecy—a woman that did foretellings —and she asked her what way would she get quit of the step-son. "It's what is keeping him so smart," says the prophecy-woman, "is the little Bullockeen out in the meadow. And let you keep a watch on him," says she, "and you'll know it's truth I'm telling," So the Queen says: "I have three daughters," says she, "and I'll send them to watch him," says she, "for the one is as sharp as an earwig, and the other is sharper again, and the third has one eye in the back of her poll that can see through every enchantment." So the first of the girls went out, but before she went the little Bullockeen says to the son: "Your step-sister will be coming to-day to watch you," says he, "and unscrew now my right horn, and take out a pin of slumber you will find under it, and when you see her coming go and play with her for a while, and put the pin of slumber into her ear and she will fall asleep." So he did as the Bullockeen told him, and he put the pin of slumber into the step-sister's ear, and she fell into a deep sleep in the grass and never woke till evening.

The next day the second of the girls went out to keep watch, where the son and the Bullockeen were eating their dinner together. But the Bullockeen rose a fog and an enchantment around them, that she could see nothing, and so she went home to her mother.

The third day the third of the daughters went out, and the son took the pin of slumber as before, and put it in her ear, and she fell asleep. But if the two front eyes were shut, the eye at the back of the poll was open. Then the Bullockeen put the fog and the enchantment around her; but if he did, the eye at the back of her poll was able to see through every enchantment, and she went back and she told the mother that the step-brother got all he could use out of the Bullockeen's horn, and that he got out of it the best dinner was in the world.

So the Queen sent again for the old prophecy, and she came, and the Queen asked her what way could she bring the King to do away with the Bullockeen. "For he will not do it for my asking," says she.

"Let you let on to be sick," says the hag, "and stop in your bed," says she, "and send for the King, and tell him there is nothing will cure you but the liver of the Bullockeen," says she.

So the Queen stopped in her bed and let on to be sick, and she sent for the King, and she said there was nothing could cure her but to kill the Bullockeen and to give her his liver. "I cannot do that," says the King; "for when that boy's mother was dying," says he, "she made a will," says he, "and she willed him nothing but the little Bullockeen in the meadow. But ask me any other thing," says he, "and I will give it."

So the Queen sent for the hag and told her that. "Let you take a little black cock is without," says the hag, "and let them kill it and take the puddings out of him," says she, "and fill it with blood, and let you put that in your mouth and squeeze it the time the King will come in, and tell him it is the heart's blood is running from you for the want of the liver of the Bullockeen," says she.

So the Queen did as she bade her, and they killed the cock and filled the pudding with blood, and the Queen put it in her mouth where she was in bed. "Oh, go run out for the King," says she, "for I am near my death." So the King came running in. "Oh," says she, "I am near my death!" says she, and she squeezes the blood out of her mouth, and the King thought it was her heart's blood was coming from her. "It will not stop," says she, "till I'll get the liver of the little Bullockeen; and let you kill him now for me," says she. "I cannot do that," says the King; and he made her the same answer as before and went out of the room.

So the Queen sent again for the old prophecy and told her all. "Haven't you a yard out there," says she, "and a wall around it," says she, "is that high a bird can hardly fly over it," says she. "And let you drive the Bullockeen in there," says she, "and put your champions around to kill it." So that was done, but when the Bullockeen saw all the champions making an attack on him, he rose up in the air, and the Queen was leaning out through the window, and he took her on his horns, and whitewashed the wall with her bones.

He called to the boy then, and the boy put a halter on him, and they rode away together where the winds never blew, and the cocks never crew, and the old boy himself never sounded his horn. And they overtook the wind that was before them, and the wind that was after them couldn't overtake them.

They came then to a great wood, and the Black Bullockeen says to the boy: "Get up now into the highest tree you can find, and stop there through the day, for I have to fight with the Red Bull that is coming against me. And unscrew my right horn," says he, "and take out the little bottle that is in it," says he, "and keep it with you; and if I am well at the end of the day," says he, "it will be as white as snow."

The Red Bull came to meet him then, and his head was as big as another's body would be; and he and the little Bullockeen went to fight together and the boy stopped up in the tree. And in the evening he looked at the little bottle, and what was in it was as white as before. So he came down, and he found the Bullockeen and got up on his back again, and they went off the same as before.

They came then to the wood where the White Bull was, and he came out to fight the Bullockeen, and all happened the same as the first day. And the boy came down from his tree and got on his back again, and they went on to another wood. And the Green Bull came to meet him this time, and the boy went up in a tree. And at evening he looked at the little bottle and it was red up to the cork. He got down then and went to look for the Bullockeen, and he found him lying on the ground at the point of death.

And the Green Bull made a great bellow, and made away and left him there. And the Bullockeen said: "I am going to leave you now," says he, "but I won't go without leaving you something. And when I am dead," says he, "cut three strips of skin off of me, from the nape of the neck to the root of the tail, and put them about your body. And you to be wearing those," says he, "they'll give you the strength of six hundred men."

So the boy sat down on the ground and cried him through three days and three nights. And after that he cut off as he was bade the three strips of the skin, and put them around his body, and they gave him the strength of six hundred men.

That now is the story of the Bullockeen, and it is a story that happened in the long ago.

THE THREE SONS

I'LL tell you a story, says the old man who was bringing fish from the sea; and after that I'll be going on to Ballinrobe, to one that has a shop there and that was reared by my grandmother. It is likely he'll give me a tasty suit of clothes. Working all my life I am; working with the flail in the barn, working with the spade at the potato tilling and the potato digging, breaking stones on the road. And four years ago the wife died, and its lonesome to be housekeeping alone.

There was a King long ago of Ireland, and he had three sons, and one of them was something silly. There came a sickness on the King, and he called his three sons, and he said to them that he had knowledge the only thing would cure him was the apples from Burnett's orchard, and he bade them to go look for them, for that orchard was in some far-away place, and no one could tell where it was.

The three sons went then, and they tackled their horses, and put on their bridles, and they set out, and went on till they came to three cross-roads. There they stopped, and they settled among themselves that each one of them would take one of the roads and go searching for the apples, and they would meet at the same place at the end of a year and a day.

The youngest son, that was a bit silly, took the crossest of the roads, and he went on till he came to a cottage by the roadside. He went in, and there was a withered old man in the house, and he said: "There is a great welcome before the King of Ireland's son!" The son was astonished at that, because he thought no one could know him. He got good treatment there, and in the course of the night he asked the old man did he know where was Burnett's garden. "I have a hundred years on me," said the old man, "and I never heard of such a place. But I have a brother," he said, "that has a hundred years more than myself, and it may be he would know," he said.

So in the morning he gave a canoe to the King's son, and it went on of itself without him turning or guiding it, till it brought him to the old man's brother, and he got a welcome there and good treatment; and in the course of the night he asked that old man did he know where was Burnett's orchard. "I do not," said he; "though I have two hundred years upon me I never heard of it.

But go on," he said, "to a brother I have that has a hundred years more than myself."

So in the morning he went into the canoe, and it went on of itself till it came to where the third old man was, that was older again than the other two, and the King's son asked did he know where was Burnett's garden. "I do not," he said, "although I have three hundred years upon me; but I will tell you how you will know it," he said. "Go on till you come to shore, where you will see a swan-gander standing by the water, and he is the one that can tell you and can bring you to it," he said. "And ask him to bring you to that garden in the name of the Almighty God."

So the King's son went on in the canoe till he came where the swan-gander was standing on the shore. "Can you tell me," says he, "where can I get the apples that are in Burnett's orchard? And can you bring me there?" he said.

"Indeed," said the swan-gander, "I am in no way obliged to your leader, or to whoever it was sent you to me and gave you that teaching. And those apples are well minded," he said, "by wolves; and the only time they ever sleep is for three hours once in every seven years. And it chances they are asleep for those three hours at this time; and so I will bring you there," he said.

With that he stretched out his wings, and he bade the King's son to get up on his back. And it was long before he could start flying with the weight that was on him; but he flew away at last, and he brought the King's son to Burnett's garden, and there was a high wall around it, but he flew over the wall, and put him down in the garden. The King's son filled his bag with the apples, and when he had done that, he went looking around, and he came to a large cottage in the garden, and he went in, and there was no one in the house but a beautiful young girl, and she asleep. So he went away; but he brought with him the gold rings and the gold garters that he saw there in the window.

He got up again on the back of the swan-gander, but it was hard for it to rise with the weight of the bag of apples. But it did rise at last, and it brought him to where the old man was that had three hundred years. And the King's son gave one of the apples to the old man, and no sooner did he eat it than his age was gone from him, and he was like a boy of fifteen years.

He went on then to the two other old men, and gave an apple to both of them, and no sooner did they eat it than they were like young boys again.

Then the King's son went back to the cross-roads, for it was the end of a year and a day, and he was the first to come there, and he fell asleep. And the two brothers came, and they saw him there,

and they stole the bag of apples from under his head, and they put
in the place of it a bag of apples that were no use at all. Then they
went on to their father's house, and they gave him the apples
they had stolen, and he was cured on the moment; but they
told him that what the youngest son was bringing to him was
poison apples, that would bring him to his death.

So the King was very angry when he heard that, and he went
to his butler and he said: "Go out to the wood where my son is,
and shoot him there, and cut him open and bring his heart here
with you on the top of the gun, and throw it to the dogs at the
door; for I will never have him, or anything belonging to him,
brought into this house," he said.

So the butler got the gun, and went out to the wood, and when
he saw the young man he was going to shoot him. "Why would
you do that?" said he. So the butler told him all the father ordered
him; and the young man said then: "Do not shoot me, but save
me. And it is what you will do," he said. "Go into the wood till
you meet with a woodcock, and shoot it, and take the heart out of
it, for that is most like the heart of a man. And bring the woodcock's heart to my father's house," he said, "and throw it there
to the dogs at the door."

So the butler did that, and spared him, and took its heart and
threw it to the dogs at the door.

It was a good while after that, the beautiful young lady came to
the King's doorway in a coach and four, and she stopped at the
door. "Send out my husband to me here," she said. So the eldest
son came out to her. "Was it you came to the garden for the apples"
says she. "It was," says he. "What things did you take notice of
in the cottage where I was?" says she.

So he began telling of this thing and that thing that never was
in it at all. And when she heard that she gave him a clout that
knocked his head as solid as any stone in the wall.

Then the second son came out, and she asked him the same
question, and he told the same lies, and she gave him another
clout that left his head as solid as any stone in the wall.

When the King heard all that, he knew they had deceived him,
and that it was the youngest son had got the apples for his cure,
and he began to cry after him and to lament that he was not living
to come back again. "Would you like to know he is living yet?"
says the butler. "I would sooner hear it than any word that ever
I heard," says the King. "Well, he is living yet, and is in the wood,"
says the butler.

When the young lady heard that, she bade the butler to bring
her where he was, and they went together to the wood, and there

they found him where he had been living on the fruits of the trees through the most of the year. So when the young lady saw him, she said: "Was it you came to the house where I was in the garden?" "It was," says he. "What things did you take notice of in it?" "Here they are," says he. And he put his hand in his pocket, and brought out the gold rings and the golden garters and the other signs he had brought away.

So she knew then he was the right one that was there, and she married him, and they lived happy ever after, and there was great rejoicing in the King of Ireland's house.

KING SOLOMON

I'LL tell you a story now, and I'll not be with you again till Christmas; and I never saw a man that could read an open book, was able to tell a story out of the mouth.

King Solomon made a great house for himself, the best that was ever seen. And there was a man passing one day, and he stopped to give a look at it—the way I might give a look at that house there. "Tell me what there is stronger and finer than that house," says King Solomon. "I don't know anything that is stronger and finer than it is," says the man. "Well," said King Solomon, "unless you can give me an answer to that by to-morrow I'll have the head struck off of you," he said.

So when the man went home, he told all that to the daughter he had, and he said he could find no answer. "I will give you an answer," says she. "Is not God stronger than that house, and isn't heaven finer than what it is?" So he went the next day and he gave that answer. "I'll give you another question," says the King then. "Tell me," says he, "what is the number of the stars of the sky! And tell me that by to-morrow," says he, "or I will strike the head off you."

So the man went home, and he could think of no answer, and he told the daughter what happened, and how King Solomon asked him to give an account of the stars in the sky. "I will give you an answer," says the daughter. "If you were to put twelve candles lighting on the top of the highest mountain," says she, "and to be looking at them, and your sight to spread on you, you wouldn't know how many you were looking at, but you might think it was hundreds. And there is no one can tell the number of the stars," says she, "or give an account of them, but God that made them."

So the man went back next day, and he gave that answer to King Solomon. "Where did you get that answer," says the king, "or who made it?" says he. "It was my daughter made it," says the man. "Bring her here till I'll have a look at her," says the king.

So the daughter was brought before him, and she was a fine comely girl, and when King Solomon saw her he took a liking to her. "Will you marry me?" says he. "I will not," says she; "for if you marry me to-day, you might throw me off again to-morrow."

I suppose she said that because she knew of him having seven hundred wives. "I will not do that," says he. "Well," says she, "I'll make a bargain with you that I'll marry you if you give me your word that the day you turn me out you'll let me carry away with me three things I'll ask for, and to have them for my own."

So King Solomon agreed to that, and she married him, and she had a child. And after a while he tired of her, and said she might go home. "I will go," says she, "but I'll bring away the three things you offered to give me." So the first thing she brought away was the child, and the second thing was a bag of gold. She came then to King Solomon. "Now," says she, "since you said I could bring away three things, it is you yourself is the third. And come with me now," she says. So when King Solomon heard that, he was afraid she would bring him with her, and that she would have power over him. So he asked her to stop with him, and so she did.

He began well and he ended badly; and Samson did the same, killing a lion that was going to eat him in the beginning, and killing himself in the end. It was through a woman that he lost his eyesight.

THE ROBINEEN

I HAVE a new wife now, says the old man who had come back from Ballinrobe; to keep my victuals ready and the door open before me. She's a quiet woman at some times, but she has a queer way in her mind at the time of the full moon, but it will pass away after. And here is a story now, and I'll word it easy to you.

There was a woman one time and she had three sons. Well, one day one of them said the quarter was too small for the three of them to be in it. "And I'll go," says he, "and I'll try to do for myself. And let you turn and make a cake for me to bring with me," says he to the mother.

The mother went at night and she baked two cakes, a big one and a small one. And when he was going to start in the morning: "Which would you sooner have now," says she, "to have the big one and my curse, or the small one and my blessing?" "I'll take the big one and your curse," says he; "the other one is too small and the road being long before me."

Well, he tripped on till he got hungry, and sat down on the brink of a lake, and he spread out a cloth for the dinner the way he would lose none of the crumbs, and he broke up a piece of the cake then and commenced eating it. The Robineen Redbreast was coming around him and he was hooshing him away. "Every crumb that will fall," says the Robineen, "it will be for me." "Every crumb that will fall," says he, "it is little enough for myself." So he hooshed away the Robineen.

When he had part of it ate, then he got dry, and he went to the lake to take a drink; and the Robineen walked to the lake before him and commenced washing herself and shaking out her wings in the lake, and she turned it all into blood instead of water. He took a drink of it, and he fell dead after taking the drink. The Robineen got people to bury him under a big stone was in it; for the Robineen was enchanted, and they say the birds of the air had talk at that time.

The two brothers then were sitting by the hearth, the same as himself, till the end of seven years. "It is this day seven years," says the second one, "that the brother went out from this. And I'll go make a poke for him. And it's as good for you," says he to the mother, "go bake a cake for the road in the morning."

Well, the mother did the same thing as before, and she made a big cake and a small cake, and asked him would he have the small one with her blessing, or the big one with her curse. "I'll have the big one with your curse," says he. So he set out, and when he came to the same place he sat down on the same stone where the brother had sat, and he spread a cloth the way any crumb that would fall, he could pick it up for himself. The Robineen came around him asking for the crumbs, and he wouldn't give them and he hooshed her away. So when he was going to the lake for a drink, she went into it before him, and spread out her wings and scattered the water, and after he took one drink of it he fell dead; and she buried the two of them under one stone, the Robineen did, the two brothers.

Well, they were fourteen years gone when the third man said he would go look for them, and the mother made two cakes the same as she made for the other two. Well, the mother told him then to take the big one or the small one; to take the big one with her curse, or to take the small one with her blessing. "There's nothing like a mother's blessing," says he. "And I'll take the small one with your blessing," he said.

It happened that he was walking till he went in the same place where the brothers were killed, and commenced eating the cake. The Robineen was coming anear him, and there wasn't a bite he would take but he would give a second bite to the Robineen. She didn't stir up the lake, but let him take his full drink, and she made a well in the lake and made wine in it and gave enough of it to him to drink. "Here is a little bush," she says then, "an enchanted bush; and give a tip to that stone there, and you can rise your two brothers." So, thanks be to God, he struck the two tips on the stone, and they rose as well as ever and as fresh. Says the Robineen: "They may be thankful to you, they would never stir out of that only for you coming."

She gave this young fellow a bag of gold for himself and his two brothers, a fine three men. They never met with the Robineen from that out. The mother's blessing is better with a small cake than her curse with a big one.

After the three brothers went home, they lived together in the house. And the Robineen had told the youngest brother to go where there was a holly-bush in the garden and to root around it. So they went out and rooted around it, and what they found was a crock of gold, and they brought it away with them. There was a little flag, now, in the top of the crock, and the flag was left aside on the grass. It happened there came after a while a poor scholar walking the road, and he took notice of the little slab, and that there was writing on it. And he was able to read the writing, and it is what it said: "The other side is as lucky as this side." So he showed that to the brothers, and they went rooting the other side, and what did they find but two more crocks of gold, the way there was one apiece for them. So there were no richer farmers in the country than those three brothers, and they got gold and divided it and scattered it.

And that is a nice story and a wonderful story, and a true thing that fell out. And Lofarey, the man that told it to me, said it was a true story, and that his own father told him he was speaking to the poor scholar that read the flag.

THE BALL OF THREAD

THERE was a young lady one time, and a young boy came to her to ask her to marry him. He gave her a pound ball of thread, and bade her to leave it on the ground, and to take the end of the thread in her hand, and when the end of it would be run out, to stamp her foot on the ground and she would come to him.

So she bought a shilling's worth of bread and a shilling's worth of apples, and she took the ball of thread as he told her. And when she stamped her foot a door opened in the ground before her, and she went in, and all she saw in the room was a dog and a cat.

So she divided the bread and the apples between them, and she gave them halves, and they were more then proud to eat that much of Ireland's bread, which they didn't get the taste of for two hundred years before.

They showed her then a store of a room where there were fifty of her sort that were after being beheaded, and gold rings on their hands. For the man was an enchanted man, and he had brought them away the same as he did herself. The cat and the dog said as she proved so well, they would hide her before she'd be in danger, for she accommodated them so well with everything. They rose up the flag that was in the fireplace, and they hid her there under it, and when the man came in the man asked did such a one come in, and they said, "No."

When he went to rest himself they opened the door and let her out, and he awoke and told the cat to ask who came in at the door. The cat made him an answer, she said: "No one but the dog, that struck against it."

So the young lady went home, and after a while he came to her again the same way, and he said he would bring her away with him. So when he was coming she invited a great quality dinner, and before he came there she told them all that had happened, and asked what should be done to him. Then some said he should be hung. But a big lord that was there said to do nothing at all to him, only to put him into a barrel of pitch and tar and to burn him altogether. But when they thought to do that and to take him they hadn't but his shadow, and he flew away out through the top of the house, and they hadn't a trace of him, and he had brought away the young lady along with him.

Her three brothers went looking for her then with the pound

ball of thread he had left. And when they stamped their foot the door opened before them, but there was no one in the house but the cat. They told him their sister was gone, and they were in dread she was killed. But he said: "She is not killed, and she is here hid where she was before." So they took up the flag of the hearth, and there she was safe and well, and having four gold rings on her hands that belonged to four of her first cousins that were beheaded in the room. The cat told them to go home, and they would meet the man easy enough. So after a while he came looking for the young lady again, and he had changed his clothes, but if he had they knew him. But the first time they fired a shot at him it did him no harm, he being but a shadow. But whatever they did, or whatever shot they put in their gun or their revolver, they shot him dead after that, and there was no more about him.

THE HORSE AND FOAL

THERE were very haunted people in the old times in Ireland, used to be bewitching one another. A living class of people they were, but it was by magic they did it.

There was a man going to the north from Mayo to sell a horse, and he was riding the horse, and the foal after them. And over beyond the wall he saw a hare running, and two black hounds hunting it. And when they came to him, the hare made a leap into his arms, and he drove away the hounds, and put it down again safe among the rocks. He went on then to the north for to sell the horse, but if he did, in the night it was stole from him.

So he went back to Mayo to see would he find it, and he was walking through the day, and when the night came he met with a house, and he went into it like any countryman might, to ask would he get a clean lodging. And there was in the house a very nice-looking young woman, and he asked could he get a lodging. "And why wouldn't you get it?" says she. "And more than that," she says, "I'll call in the husband, and he'll go find the horse you have lost and the foal. And you don't know me," she says; "but I am the woman you saved, and that had been turned into a hare, and for sixteen years I was away in that shape."

So she did what she promised, and he was deserving of it; for wouldn't another man have kept the hare when he got it, but something stuck in him that he didn't. And wasn't it a terrible thing in those times that women could be turned into hares? And it was only a black hound could come up with them.

THE WOMAN THAT WAS A GREAT FOOL

THERE was a woman was a great fool. She had meal to sift one day, and the hens were bothering her, coming in over the door. And it was outside in the field she went sifting it, that it was brought away with a blast of wind that rose, till there wasn't one grain left on the top of another, but it was brought away with the wind into the fields and over the grass. And when the husband came back in the evening he asked where was it, and it was all spent. "Sure you have money in the bag to buy more," says she. "I have not," says he; "for what is in the bag I have to keep for the Grey Scrape of the Spring."

Well, the next day an old beggarman came asking for money, and when the woman looked at him and saw that he was grey: "That should be the Grey Scrape of the Spring," she said. And she gave him all the money was in the bag.

When the husband heard that, he didn't say much, for he was a quiet man. But he went and he killed the cow that was all he had left, and he cut it up and put it in a barrel, and salt on it. "That will be enough to grease the cabbage anyway," says he.

So the next day the wife brought out every bit of the beef, and she put a bit of it on the top of every head of cabbage was in the garden. Well, when the night came and they were in bed, there came a thousand dogs fighting for the meat was in the garden, and barking, and calling and roaring. And when the husband went out they had it brought away, and all the cabbage destroyed and broken.

So he said then it was as good for them to go wandering, and he went out of the house, and the woman following him. "Let you draw the door after you," says he—that is, that she should close it. But what she did was to rise it off the hinges, and to draw it after her along the road till they came to a wood. And they went into the branches of a tree to pass the night, and she bringing the board with her.

It happened there came some robbers under the tree, dividing a great deal of gold and silver they were after robbing from a castle. And when the man and the woman saw that, they dropped the door down on them with a great noise, and the robbers were affrighted and ran away, leaving all they had robbed after them. And the man and the woman got it for themselves, and they were rich from that day.

THE BLACK BULLOCKEEN DIES.

THE THIRD THING I'LL BE TAKING IS YOURSELF.

THE DANES

I will tell you about the Danes, said the Poet's son; and it was my father that broke down Raftery in the latter end.

There was a man one time set out from Ireland to go to America or some place; a common man looking for work he was. And something happened to the ship on the way, and they had to put to land to mend it. And in the country where they landed he saw a forth, and he went into it, and there he saw the smallest people he ever saw; and they were the Danes that went out of Ireland, and it is foxes they had for dogs, and weasels were their cats.

Then he went back to get into the ship, but it was gone away, and he left behind. So he went back into the forth and a young man came to meet him, and he told him what had happened. And the young man said: "Come into the room within, where my father is in bed; for he is out of his health, and you might be able to serve him." So they went in, and the father was lying in the bed, and when he heard it was a man from Ireland was in it he said: "I will give you a great reward if you will go back and bring me a thing I want out of Castle Hacket Hill; for if I had what is there," he said, "I would be as young as my own son." So the man consented to go, and they got a sailing ship ready, and it is what the old man told him, to go back to Ireland. "And buy a small pig in Galway," he said, "and bring it to the mouth of the forth at Castle Hacket and roast it there. And inside the forth there is an enchanted cat that is keeping guard there, and it will come out. And here is a shot-gun and some cross-money," he said, "that will kill any fairy or any enchanted thing. And within in the forth," he said, "you will find a bottle and a rack-comb, and bring them here to me," he said.

So the man did as he was told, and he bought the pig and roasted it at the mouth of the forth, and out came the enchanted cat, and it having hair seven inches long. And he fired the cross-money out of the shotgun, and the cat went away and he saw it no more. And he got the bottle and the rack, and brought them back to the old man. And he drank what was in the bottle, and racked his hair with the rack, and he got young again, as young as his own son.

And when there is a marriage among the Danes, they put down the land they have in Ireland with whatever else they have, for they expect to come back and to own the country again some day. But whether they will or not, I don't know.

The Danes were surely small men, or how could they live in those little rooms and passages in the raths? I'd have to stoop myself down when I'd go into them. They had the whole country once, and they used to make beer out of the tops of the heather the same way the bees draw honey out of it. And it was on St. John's Night the people lighted wisps and turned them out of Ireland, and that's the reason the wisps are burned ever since.

CAILLEAC-NA-CEARC

I THINK I didn't tell you the story of Cailleac-na-Cearc, the
Woman of the Hens, says the old man with the new wife; and how
she committed sin.

It was one day they rose up, herself and her twelve children,
and there was not bit or drop in the house, and the height of the
door of frost and snow was in it; and she sent the husband out to
see could he get firing with a little hatchet he had.

And when he went out he got directions to cut a certain tree.
And there came out of the tree to him as much as he could carry
of lumber of the best of stuff, and he brought it home to the wife.

Well, after a while she bade him go again to the tree and cut it.
And there came from it the same lumber of provisions and gold
and money and everything they wanted. And the third time she
sent him to cut the tree, and the tree spoke to him that time, and
it said: "You may take what you can this time, but let you never
come near me again." And he brought back more than would fill
the corners of the house. And he said to the wife, that was enough.

But she made him go the fourth time, for women is awful, and
she wanted to get all that she could; and only for her bidding he
didn't like to draw back to the tree. And that time the tree spoke
to him again, and it said: "You have full and plenty, and you'll
see the way your missus is, and you going back to the house."
For she was covetous and had no patience, and it was by the
Almighty God's will he made a hen of her, and twelve chickens
of her twelve children. And she went scraping in the face of the
dunghill, and she never left doing that till the day of judgment,
picking for her chickens that stopped small as they were always.

When she had too much she wasn't pleased till she got more,
and so she couldn't keep it and had nothing at all left her in the
heel of the hunt.

I suppose it was God that made the provision within in the tree.
For the man was holy. Did he mind seeing his children turned
into chickens? He did not. He was a born saint, and it is likely it
was a saint talked with him abroad at the tree; and he had full and
plenty while he lived; and the day he died the gates of heaven were
open, and it was as a white pigeon that he went in through them.
That now is a true story, and that is a thing that surely happened.

THE GOATS

THERE was a girl had a sweetheart that was called Shawn Shamus. And through the crying of the Banrighean-na-breena he was brought away into a forth. The girl went to the forth looking for him, and outside of it she saw the Banrighean, the Queen, sitting and she combing her hair, and having a blue dress on her like those flowers that grow in the fields. "Will you give me back Shawn Shamus?" says the girl. "I will not," says the Queen. And she went on talking for a while, the girl asking and the Queen refusing. And at the last the Queen said: "I will give him to you if you will bring me a hundred barrels of sixpenny money, a hundred fillies all of the one colour, a hundred spotted cows, a hundred ganders and a fleet of geese; a hundred slips and a hundred pigs, a hundred goats that are without damage or roguery." So the girl went looking for all those, and she brought every one of them to the Queen of the forth except the goats, for she could not get one that was honest, they are all full of roguery. Everything else but the goats she brought. So the Queen gave up Shawn Shamus, and they married and lived happy.

THE CURIOUS WOMAN

THERE will be no eating in the other world, says the red-haired man sitting at the door. "But there is a tree in it with twelve sorts of fruit, and what would that be for if we were not to eat it?" Well, the first man that went eating fruit made a bad hand of it. He bethought of himself and it going down, and it stopped in his throat and gave us that lump in it ever since. Isn't that a terrible thing for a man to have? But as to the woman, what she ate stopped down, and so it would if she ate another along with it. Women are terrible for eating things. Women are curious, and that is what led her to it. And besides that it was nice-looking, and women like to have nice things. A woman to see a lady, she would want all she would be wearing for herself—red stockings and shoes and dresses, and even to umbrellas.

There was an old couple were past working and they went travelling the roads, and they met a King that had a palace he had no use for, and he said they could have the use of it. So he brought them in and put them into a big room, and there was a big table with every sort of food on it, and he bade them use what they could of what was there. But there was a board of the table he bade them not to touch, and the reason was he had put a mouse under it that would tell him every word they would say.

Well, when they had ate all they could, the woman began to say she would look what was under that board. "Do not," says the man, "and the King after telling you not to touch it." "Sorra fear he to know of it," says she. But he wouldn't let her do it that night or the next night, but the third night she put out her hand and rose up the board, and out ran the mouse. And they tried to catch it, but you may believe they were not able to come up with it. And so when the King saw they had the board shifted, he turned them out of the palace and they were as poor as before.

THE MISFORTUNE—

"THERE WAS A MAN THAT SORROW CALLED HIS FRIEND"

I HAVE a nice wonderful story now picked upout. From Mike McCarthy I got it where I was two days weeding potatoes. He had a road of ridges sowed and they were ate with the weeds and the dirt. Ninepence a day was all I got, but with that my support and my bed.

There was a man that misfortune followed through the whole course of his life, and his sheep used to go straying and to be stripped of half their wool. And what he'd do in the morning he wouldn't have the trace of it at night, and he never could spare anything for the misfortune was always following him.

He was going along the road one day to see could he make out a bite to nourish his nine children, and he took notice of a shadow that was walking beside him. "Are you going far along with me?" says he to the shadow. He darted that question on him. "I am going with you since the day you were born" says the shadow that was the Misfortune "and I will be going with you till the day you will be buried." "If that is so" says the poor man "it's as good for me to be buried to-day." So he took a spade and he went into a grave-yard and the Misfortune was watching with him. And he started digging a hole and when he had it dug, he says to the Misfortune: "Let you lie down in it till I'll see will it be wide enough and will it be my fit". So the Misfortune lay down in the grave, and when he did, my fellow closed it over him and turned the sod on him and went away and left him. And when he went home he saw a ball of thread was tied on to the treddle of the spade. And the wife brought it to the weaver, and it wasn't any size at all by looking at it but he made sixty yards of flannel from the thread, the length that would cover a house. It is likely now that was the wool used to be stripped from his sheep by the Misfortune or some other fairies that were enchanted, it is how they returned him the compliment. And this fellow that the Misfortune used to be following always was getting rich every day, and the luck he didn't get in the morning he would get it in the evening, and the luck he wouldn't get in the evening he'd get it the next morning.

This man now had a rich brother who had a wife, and though

the brother was so poor and nine in family they wouldn't look at him, there was no charity about them. And when they saw the poor man to be getting rich the wife was vexed and she begrudged him to be rising in the world. So she drew to his wife and she picked out of her what happened, and that the Misfortune was closed in the grave, and the place where it was.

She brought men then to the graveyard and she set them around and bade them dig till they took the sod off the Misfortune and he rose again and stood up out of the grave. "Go back now," says she "till you'll follow the man you were always following before." "I will not," says he, "but it is yourself I will follow from this out." So he turned around and he followed the rich man's wife, and all she had and her husband had, it reduced from them from that time. And she would be coming on her knees to the man the Misfortune went from, begging the bite she would eat, and nothing at all remained to her, but all went from her in the heel.

THE WELL OF HEALING[1]

THERE was a King's son, and the King fell sick and there was nothing could cure him only three drops from a bottle of the water of the well that the cure of the world was in. He was seven years on the bed and nothing was to cure him only that.

An enchanted lady come then out from a forth (I suppose she was something to them) and she told the King's son to start and to look for that well on the next Monday morning and to bring back a bottle of that water. "Oh," says the son, "how can I get that?" "No one ever," says she, "got a sup of that water or brought their legs out of it but by starting a Monday morning. For there is a queen that is minding the well" she said "and there are forty five beagles beside her. But herself and the beagles sleep for five hours every Friday and that is the day you must come to it," she says. "For there are five days of the week she wouldn't sleep at all or the beagles either, but only watching the well. And it is only a slate coloured horse," she says "that will bring you there." Why was that Queen put there? Maybe she was put there like any young lady that would be flied away to mind that well until the term would be out, and a King's son would come to give her the marks and tokens.

So he walked all the fairs of Ireland, and he couldn't meet with a slate horse and he came home, and the king was ready to die all the time.

So when the enchanted lady came again, he told her he was after walking all the fairs of Ireland and he couldn't get the colour of the horse she told him. "And I'm as bad now as ever I was," the King said. "I'll get you a horse of that colour," says she. So she came to him the day she appointed and took out a purse and took out the stones that were in it. He never could have got to the well but for the stones that were in it and he was told to beat three taps of a rod on every one. And they were horses that were enchanted, and when he hit the first with a rod, it was a red one. And he would not use that and the second was cream and the third was slate. And that was the one he took in the heel and if it was not for the colour of it he would not have got the water. He went then and when he got to the place there was thirteen feet of a demesne wall around it, and he faced the horse at it, and jumped it, for no horse was able to jump it but that slate coloured one. That demesne wall surrounded about the wood and he saw the young queen sleeping on the brink of the well, and a gold

[1] See Appendix.

bed around her and the forty five beagles on each side of her, minding herself and the well. He went within five yards of the well and he tied the horse to a palm tree.

Well, he stole a march then and went to the well and brought the bottle of water. He was only just on horseback then when one of the beagles wakened and found the scent and they went on his track, but they stopped at the demesne wall and they weren't able to jump it and you'd hear them in the West Indies roaring.

Well, he went home and gave the three drops of the water to the King that was his father; and the King that was after being seven years in the bed rose up the age of fifteen years, he was so supple and so good.

Then the enchanted woman that told him about the well and give him the horse, came for the horse back and for the remainder of the water. Well he gave her the remainder of the water and the horse back. And it cured three kings who were in relationship to the lady that was enclosed within in the forth, where there is a good many of them. No sooner she had it got than the King fell back in the same form again. "Well, what will I do now?" he said. "You are as bad as the first time," he says to his father that was the King.

Well, when the father yielded so much, the enchanted woman told him he must go and get another bottle from the well. "If I got all Ireland's ground" he said, "and England along with it I'll not go there again." "Ah, there'll be no fear of you" says the enchanted woman, "for I'll give you the same horse you had before."

So he started on Monday morning and he went to the well and filled his bottle again and the young lady minded the well was asleep. Well, she felt him going and she wakened and when she saw him that he was a fine looking young gentleman she didn't want to free him; no, he was such a fine man.

He came to the demesne wall and the horse jumped the wall and no sooner the horse had the wall jumped than the Queen came and jumped it after him; and went behind him on the horse's back and squeezed him into her heart and fell in love with him on the very minute. Well, then he came to his father's palace and gave him three drops of the water, and he was as well as ever again. And when he waked he fell in love with the young lady on the very minute and was very proud of the son to have such a lady coming home. Then the young King's son married her and they lived all together. And the beagles remained there minding the well all the time and herself and the young King's son went there once in the year to look at it. And she put a gateman there and gave him in charge to keep the beagles fed.

202

THE TAILOR

THERE was a King was building a castle, and every night all that was built in the day would be knocked again, and they could not know what was doing it. The King offered four hundred pounds to any man that would go and mind the castle that night, and there came a tailor and he went to the King and said he would watch it. So he watched and there came two giants in the night time, and the tailor got a stone and gave one of them a clout on the head that he fell dead and the other ran away. And the tailor cut off the skull and brought it back to the King.

The next night the giant that ran away came back to the castle and another brother that was a giant with him.

There rose an argument between them, and the tailor struck a stone on one of the giants and the giant turned around at his own brother and said it was he had done it. "I know well you want to kill me" says he "as it was you that killed the eldest brother yesterday and that you want to kill myself in like manner" says the third giant. So he took a stone and knocked him dead, and away with him, and the tailor cut the skull off of him and brought it back to the King's court.

The third night the third giant came back, and the tailor spoke friendly to him and said he was the best giant in Ireland to be able to behead his two brothers. He brought the tailor home then as a comrade in the place of the brothers. They started then to eat a meal of stirabout against one another to see which of them would eat the most. But the tailor was smart and there was no end to his planning and he took a sheepskin and sewed it the same as you might sew a petticoat till it was in the shape of a bag, and he put it in under his vest. Then himself and the giant started eating and after a while the tailor says "I can give myself a prod of a knife to let out all I'm after eating." So he took out his knife and gave a prod to the sheepskin and all the stirabout fell out. The giant took a knife then and gave himself a prod in the same way, killed himself and there was an end of him, and the tailor brought back his skull to the King.

He went then to the house where the giant's mother was, and she told him her three sons were killed. "I will take service with you so" says the tailor. "What could you do?" says the mother "Tell me what actions they used to be doing" says he. There was a sledge lying on the ground and the tailor was looking at it but he could not so much as lift it. "They used to be throwing that sledge five hundred yards" says the mother. So the tailor went as if to lift it. "What are you thinking to do with it?" says the mother. "I am taking my aim" says he "Where I am going to throw it into the East Indies." (He that wasn't able to stir it off the ground.) "Do not, but leave it where it is," calls out the mother, "for that is where the fourth son I have is at this time, and it is likely it might kill him." "What other actions used they to be doing?" says the tailor. "They used to go into the wood below, and every-one of them would bring me three carloads of timber on his back." "Bring me there so" says the tailor. So when they got to the wood, the tailor began going from one tree to another tree till he didn't leave one without putting a hack in it. "Why are you doing that?" says the mother, "Ah, where's the use bringing in carloads," says he, "it's as good for me to bring the whole wood at the one time." He was knotting one tree to another, and three boxes of matches would put enough of weight on the tailor, he was no good at all, but his talk. So when the mother heard that, she was in dread of him, and she said she would go away from there and would leave him all that belonged to herself and her three sons. So when he had banished the mother and killed the three giants he went back to the King and the King was able to build his castle then, and he gave the tailor two thousand pounds. And the tailor was no good at all, but the worst man God ever put breath in but he let on to be able to do so much. For tailors are very smart with their tongue and they will make you a promise and will not keep it. And it is tailors and weavers and carpenters that are the smuggest liars in Ireland.

THE TWO BROTHERS

I AM thinking I never told you, my lady, the story of the rich brother and the poor brother and it is but a couple of words.

There was a rich man having plenty but he had no child, and the brother he had was very poor and he had nine in his family. Their mother that had four hundred pounds took herself to live with the rich man, and it happened that she died, and she left all to the man that had full and plenty and nothing at all to the man that was poor.

Well, in the night time the poor man was talking with the wife, and they didn't know in the world what way could they live. "Go out now," says the wife, for women can give good advice, "and rise up your mother out of the grave. And as every corpse is stiff, bring it to the brother's house and put it leaning against the door the way it will fall on whoever will first open the door in the morning." "Begob, that's not a bad thought at all," says the poor man. So they made up their mind to that and he went and rose his mother out of the grave and put her against the door. And the first that opened it in the morning was the housekeeper and she saw the dead corpse there in the shroud and it fell on her and she gave a screech and ran to tell her master. "It is my mother left the grave," says he, "where she left no share to my brother that is poor and that was a great wrong to him." So he sent for the brother and he gave him the half of the fortune the mother left, two hundred pounds, and bade him to put her back in the grave. "And you'll get the other two hundred," says he, "at whatever time I will be satisfied she will not leave the grave again." So he took and buried her and heaped plenty of earth over her, and he got the rest of the money and he put it to good use, he reared his family. That now is a true story, as true as that I'm sitting here.

THE TWELVE GIANTS AND
THE GIANT FROM THE FAR OFF INDIES

Now I'll tell you a story and I'll word it easy for you. There was twelve of the giants some time ago in Ireland, and there was no one could correspond with them. And there was a giant came from the far off Indies, the West Indies, to fight the twelve of them.

And so they put the best man of them driving the cows, and the second best that was called Finn MacCumhail they made a child of him in the cradle, and put a brass cap on him.

Well, so when the Giant came, no one was in the house only Finn's mother and the child, that was in the cradle. She baked a cake and she put a large griddle in the centre of the cake. When this big giant came to try their strength, they were all gone; they were run home afraid of him. He would have been able to conquer the best of them, and they were the best giants ever counted in Ireland.

Well the giant's mother left him down a dinner and there was the big cake with the griddle in the centre of it, and the first bite he took, it knocked a tooth out of him. "Is this the kind they do be using?" he says to the mother. "Yes," she says, "the child in the cradle, it is the same bread he is using," she says. "Has he teeth?" says the giant. "Put your finger in his mouth," says the mother, "and you'll know he hasn't but the gum." He tried him then; he put his finger in the mouth and the child when he got it, he took the top of the finger from him, so he was well wounded.

After dinner then he says: "What are their actions they do be trying?" "Well," she says, "there is a brown stone there abroad, and it is their exercise after dinner to throw it over the lodge and not to let it come to the ground till they will take it in their hands," she says, she knowing the twelve of them could hardly take the stone. So the giant that came from the far Indies took it and put it over the lodge and before it was on the ground he thought to be under it to catch it in his hand and it came down on his side and broke three ribs off him, and that was the third wound he got.

He was sorrowful enough after the day's end and he said he'd turn home, and he hard wounded.

And the one he met on the road was the cow boy, the best man of all that was and he driving one bull only to twelve cows. The giant came to attack him, and said he'd bring home the bull. "By

God you won't," says the cow boy; "because I won't let him go with you."

Well, they caught the bull then, one by each horn, they caught him by the horns keeping him from each other. With the force the two had, they tore him from the tip of his nose to the top of his tail, and they had a half each of him. They tore the bull alive.

The cow boy went home, and he had only half the bull going home on his back and the twelve cows out before him. "Where is the other half of the bull?" says Finn MacCumhail's mother, "Only for I was a good man" says her son, "you wouldn't see half itself."

Well, word came that the Giant was coming back to try them again. "Well, if he do, take my advice," says Finn. "You'll hire the King's son from Ireland, that was learning action where that child was born."

So they wrote for the King's son from Ireland and he wouldn't settle with them unless he'd get the young lady, that was a sister of the child was in the cradle, to be married to him, and before they parted they gave consent.

And in six months then the giant came again to see them, and they spent four days and four nights and two swords, the King's son and the giant fighting. And after the four days and the four nights, the breath left the pair of them and they died on the spot, the King's son and the giant.

The young lady that was married to him there, she had some charm and she was so fond of him she got a quill and a little skillet like, and she lifted down in the little pot whatever stuff was in the pot.

Well, she kept rubbing him about his eyes and about his mouth till the life came again in him as well as ever. He was a King's son from Ireland.

"Well now," says he when he got his life again, "I'm seventeen years gone" he says, "and I'll take a trip to Ireland to see my father and mother."

So he did, and there was new regulations there, no man could go inside the gate without having a ticket.

There was a new king and new queen married in the house in it, in his dwelling. He had no ticket, and every man that thought to stop him, he broke the locks and broke the gates and struck them a clout each, and put their head as solid as any stone that was in the double wall.

Well, my lady, he went in, and he saw the father, the old King, sitting on one side, and the mother sitting the other side, and they badly dressed.

He didn't let them know he was their son, and he wasn't long with them when the old King called for a drink, and he sitting on a chair near the fire. The butler came out and took a black saucepan and gave him a drink out of it.

Well, the old King refused it, and when he didn't take it, the butler dashed saucepan and all in the face of the old King, when he refused to take it.

When the son saw what he did, his blood boiled, he got up off the chair where he was sitting and he struck the butler a clout; and with the sweep he gave him he put his head as solid as any stone was in the earth. He then caught his father and put him on his right knee, rubbed him and wiped him with his pocket-handkerchief. When that was done he caught the mother and done the same with her.

He went in the parlour then where the young King and Queen were. "Who gave you the authority" he says, "to sit here and be not treating my father and mother the same as ye are?" They couldn't answer or give any excuse, whatever way they came in it. He did the same with the young King and Queen and put their heads in as solid as any stone in the wall. "And let you take and make a cake for me" says he to the mother. He had them all banished then and he had the house kept for his father and mother and his lady, and all that was in it. That is all I know about it, and that is one of the old stories of Ireland.

THE KING'S SON FROM INDIA
AND THE DARK KING

I CAN'T tell it well but I'll stagger it as well as I can. There was a Dark King and he was seven years that he never spoke a word and never made a laugh and was without saying yes or no.

There came the King's son from India and asked him why was he seven years without speaking a word. And he said it was because the time he was beaten in a battle and got three wounds in the skull and in the elbow and the heel he lost the use of his knee. "And it was at that time," he said "my seven sons and my seven packs of hounds were lost from me." So the King's son that was the best in the world, went looking for them. And he found where there were big stones, and a charm rose out of the stones and there came out the seven sons as young as they were before and the seven packs of hounds, and he brought them back to the Dark King. Himself got well in the heel and the elbow, and the knee and the head got as well as ever they were.

"You can take my daughter now," said the Dark King, "and you can join and be married to one another." So they married and wedded together.

Then the King's son from India got a little canoe of a boat to go in through the rivers from Ireland to India, he had so much of a charm he could bring it through all the world. And he brought the Dark King's daughter to India along with him.

THE GOLD OF IRELAND

THERE was one of the Danes was in the East Indies and he went from that to the West Indies, and when he came there he had not got his razor for he forgot it in the East Indies. So he sent his brother for the razor and he went and he got it in the East Indies, and when he was there they gave him a pot of broth to drink, and when he had drunk it there was not a place in Ireland had hidden gold in it but he knew where it was and the name of it. So when he came back to the brother he told him about the pot of broth, and that he knew where to find all the hidden gold in the whole of Ireland. The brother put down a plate of meat before him. "Let you eat that" says he. So he ate the meat and when he took his head from the plate all he had learned drinking the broth had gone from him as if he never knew it before.

That is why you might hear the old people saying, "If it wasn't for the meat the brother would be very good."

NOTE

I HAVE not changed a word in these stories as they were told to me, but having heard some of them in different versions from different old people, I have sometimes taken a passage or a phrase from one and put it in another where it seemed to fit. *The Seven Fishers* for instance, the beginning of which I have given as told by the old man of a hundred years, drifted into the adventures of *Shawneen* and of *The Bullockeen*, and I took another ending for it; and the story of *Shawneen*, begun in a workhouse, was continued at my own door by a piper from County Kerry. I have only once, in *The Seven Fishers*, taken a few sentences from a story told, not to me, but to another. I tell this, because folk-lorists in these days are expected to be as exact as workers at any other science.

As to the substance of the stories, there is a hint in *Shawneen* of Perseus and Andromeda, and in *The Three Sons* of the Garden of the Hesperides, and of Eden itself in *The Curious Woman*. And who can say whether these have travelled from east to west, or from west to east, for the barony of Kiltartan, in common with at least three continents, holds fragments of the wonder tales told in the childhood of the world.

A. G.

APPENDIX

Lady Gregory had prepared for a second edition of The Kiltartan Wonder Book *and had loosely inserted in her own copy a further six stories to be included in it. All but one required little or no editing, only the correction of typing errors. The Well of Healing required quite a lot of work as it existed in two variant forms which Lady Gregory obviously had not had time to work into one.*

In order to cause no gap in the story, the editors have combined the two versions, keeping as far as possible to the author's style. In order to let readers see both versions of the story as typed out by Lady Gregory, they are given below.

THE WELL OF HEALING

THERE was a King's son, and the King fell sick and there was nothing could cure him only a bottle of the water of the well that the cure of the world was in. He was seven years on the bed and nothing was to cure him only that.

An enchanted lady came then, out from a forth, I suppose she was something to them, and she told the King's son to start and to look for that well on the next Monday morning and to bring back a bottle of that water. "Oh," says the son, "how can I get that?" "No one ever" says she "got a sup of that water or brought their legs out of it but by starting a Monday morning. For there is a Queen minding the well" she said "that is called the Queen of Shot, because she has three revolvers besides her and nine beagles on each side of her. But herself and the beagles sleep for five hours every Friday, and that is the day you must come to it" she said "for there are five days of the week that she wouldn't sleep at all or the beagles either, but only watching the well. And it is only a slate-coloured horse she says that will bring you there". "Why was that Queen put there?" Maybe she was put there like any young lady that would be flied away to mind that well until the term would be out, and that a King's son would come to give her the marks and tokens.

So he walked all the fairs of Ireland, and he couldn't meet with a slate horse, and he came home and the King was ready to die all the time.

So when the enchanted lady came again he told her he was after walking all the fairs of Ireland and he couldn't get the colour of the horse she told him. "And I'm as bad now as ever I was" he said. "I'll get you a horse of that colour" says she. So she came to him the day she appointed stones there were in it. He went then, and when he got to the place there was thirteen feet of a demesne wall around it, and he faced the horse at it, and it jumped it, but no horse was able to jump it but that slate coloured one. That demesne wall surrounded about the wood, and the Queen was there asleep, and nine beagles on each side of her, minding herself and the well. He was within five yards of the well and he tied the horse to a palm tree.

Well, he stole a march then and went to the well and brought the bottle of water. He was only just on to horseback then when one of the beagles wakened and found the scent and they went on his track, but they stopped at the demesne wall because it was thirteen feet of a wall and they weren't able to jump it, and you'd hear them in the West Indies roaring.

Well, he went home and he gave the three drops of the water to the King that was his father; and the King that was after being seven years in the bed rose up the age of fifteen years, he was so souple and so good.

This enchanted woman that told him and gave him the horse, came for the horse back and for the remainder of the water. Well, he gave her the remainder of the water and the horse back. And it cured three Kings in relationship to the lady that was enclosed within in the forth, where there is a good many of them. No sooner she had it got than the King fell back in the same form again. "Well what will I do now?" he says. "You are as bad as the first time" he says to his father that was the King.

Well, when the father yielded so much, the enchanted woman told him he must go and get another bottle of water from the well. "If I got all Ireland's ground" he said, "and England along with it I'll not go there again." "Ah, there'll be no fear of you" says the enchanted woman "for I'll give you the same horse you had before."

So he started on Monday morning and he went to the well and filled his bottle again, and the young lady minding the well was fast asleep. Well, she felt him going and she wakened and when she saw him that he was a fine looking young gentleman she didn't want to free him; no, my lady, he was such a fine young man.

He came to the demesne wall, and the horse jumped the wall, and no sooner the horse had the wall jumped than the Queen of Shot came and jumped it after him, she did, my lady, and went behind him on the horse's back and squeezed him into her heart and fell in love with him on the very minute. Well, then he came to his father's palace and gave him three drops of the water, and he was as well as ever again, and when he waked he fell in love with the young lady on the very minute, and was very proud of the son to have such a lady coming home. Then the young King married her, and they lived all together. And the beagles remained there minding the well all the time, and herself and the young King went there once in the year to look at it. And she put a gateman there and gave him in charge to keep the beagles fed.

· · · · · ·

Niland says Mike Loegary's story was a hard one, and he only heard a bit of it about a young lady that wanted a cure for a King's daughter and that was a drink of water from a well that the cure of the world was in.

She never could have got to it only for the horse, stones that were in it and to beat three taps of a rod on every one. And they were horses that were enchanted, and when he hit the first with the rod it was a red one. And she wouldn't like that, and the second was cream and the third was snuff (slate). And that was the one she took in the heel, and if it was not for the colour of it she would not have got the water. She went to a man and she asked him what way would she get to the well, and he says "you have no getting of that no more than you'd cut your right hand." Then she went to another man that lived nearer to the well. "Well, you have luck with you" says he, "for the three queens that are minding the well do not sleep but once in seven years, and then they sleep for three hours. And it is just at this time the sleep is on them" he said.

So she came to the well and she leaped the forty-five beagles and the hundred of soldiers that were minding it, and she saw the three queens asleep and the young queen sleeping on the brink of the well and a golden bed around her. So she brought away a drink of the water from the well and cured the King's daughter.

If it wasn't for the horse that was enchanted she could not have crossed the blazing mountain or the mountain of needles. But the horse as he leaped the fiery mountain quenched the fire, and the needles of the other mountain, he turned their points face downwards.

(*Written along the margin are the words* "*Insert in Well of Healing.*")